The Little Book of Narcissism

The Essential Guide to Stop Wasting
Time and Energy on the Narcissist in Your Life

Dr. Sharon Kelly

ISBN: 978-1-735-0123-1-5

Disclaimer: Sharon Kelly is a Licensed Clinical Psychologist in the State of Pennsylvania. The materials and information offered by Kelly in this book are intended to encourage and to teach skills that support attitudinal and relational change.

This book is not intended to replace or simulate medical or psychological advice of any kind. The contents of this book are intended to be used as an adjunct to a rational and responsible mental healthcare program prescribed by a mental healthcare practitioner. The author and publisher are in no way liable for any use or misuse of this material.

A Note on Privacy: Confidentiality and discretion are the highest priorities in Sharon Kelly's work. Because of this, Kelly has taken real life types of events to create simulated stories and characters in this book. Any resemblance to any specific person or persons is purely coincidental.

Visit Dr. Kelly at www.villagepsychology.com

CRICKLEWOOD PRESS

Dedicated to those who have suffered
from narcissistic abuse or neglect.

A Note to Readers

This book is intended to provide information about narcissistic behaviors and tendencies. It also explores types of interpersonal dynamics relative to individuals with narcissistic personalities. It is not a substitute for professional mental health services. If you are at risk for emotional or psychiatric issues, it is important for you to seek professional support services. Services and resources can be accessed from psychologists, support groups, psychiatrists, and other mental health providers.

All vignettes offered here are simulated to reflect real life dynamics. All characters and stories included in this book are fictitious. Any resemblance to specific person or persons is purely coincidental.

Acknowledgments

To Sandra Volgger-Balazinski, my forever confidante, for being a devoted friend during our best and worst moments and for always supporting my dreams.

To Catherine Quillman, respected author, journalist, artist, and friend, for her help editing and for her gracious support of my creative pursuits.

To Fred Weyman, the most talented photographer alive, for his help with the design cover and for his assistance during the coronavirus crisis, so that my energy could be consistently directed toward this project .

To Dr. Jenn McIntosh, my anam cara and world class psychologist, for being my role model for grace in balancing motherhood and the practice of psychology.

To Bob Lohr, valued friend and wise counsel, for providing light at the end of a dark tunnel.

To Jofke, the talented graphic designer, for his original image of the threatening narcissus flower for the cover.

And to my children—Paul, for always impressing me with his focused discipline, calm confidence, and sense of humor. And to Jill, for her ability to bring lightness, enthusiasm, and fun into any project.

Finally, to my friends—especially Patti Ferri, Janice Christian, Micheal Stancato, Joyce Makansi, Cindi Wood and Diane Zappas for their encouragement and useful feedback on this project.

Introduction

I t was an epiphany. You went online and actually found an explanation for the crazy, crippling, toxic feelings you've been experiencing because of a particular individual in your life. It all made sense. The mother, the father, the sibling, the politician, or the co-worker that makes you feel like you are crazy . . . is a *narcissist.*

It's just the beginning, however, since you've been dazed and demoralized by this person for so long. You may shocked to discover that there are others who have shared this same insane, dehumanizing experience as you have. Once discovered, it is almost impossible to stop seeking information. It's just so validating to realize that *you are not crazy.*

The information itself can be almost as addicting as the actual narcissist. Your thoughts became consumed by this new revelation. You might even begin replacing your addiction *to the narcissist* for an addiction to information *about the narcissist.*

Most books on the topic of narcissists—as well as many therapists—conclude that the only real solution is to cut them out of your life entirely. Given the damage and abuse of which they are capable, I don't necessarily disagree. Unfortunately, many partners, family members, and coworkers may not want to—or believe that they cannot—disconnect from the narcissist in their lives.

As you develop a basis understanding of this topic, you will realize that the narcissist in your life is only doing what narcissists typically do. It has nothing to do with you. Your response can only make a difference in your own life, and in the way you feel about yourself. In rare instances, depending upon the specific narcissist, there may be some hope that the horrific behaviors can be shaped or influenced. Don't necessarily count on that, but know with a certainty that when you change the way you feel about yourself, overall change will be inevitable.

Narcissists bring out our weaknesses and vulnerabilities. At first, we might be on a pedestal but sooner or later, we will be devalued. Over time this only gets worse until we no longer feel like ourselves anymore. We have been depleted and beaten down. The narcissist eventually has full control over our thoughts and our emotions. They thrive off our weakest moments and are threatened by our strengths.

When you become increasingly more self-respecting, confident, and secure with yourself—the behaviors of a narcissist become naturally intolerable. The narcissist must change because the manipulation, lies, and scapegoating no longer work. The relationship proceeds in a more stable and respectful manner. Depending upon the developmental stage and level of severity of the narcissism demonstrated, this positive outcome may only result in the rarest of cases.

In an alternate and more likely scenario, you have come to understand the behaviors of the narcissist. You became aware of your role in the interpersonal dynamics between the two of you. As you begin to observe these patterns without reaction, your own personal strength emerges. The drama and nonsense gets old and stale. The decision to disconnect becomes obvious.

Partners of narcissists who enter therapy for professional guidance and support are often very well-informed ahead of time. What turns out to be most helpful in therapy are the insights clients develop *about themselves* and the interpersonal dynamics that occur between them and the narcissist. The key to ultimate freedom is dependent upon that broader understanding along with the willingness to adapt accordingly.

The information offered in these pages are by no means exhaustive on the subject of narcissism. It is intentionally focused on essential information on the topic of narcissism and insights about interpersonal dynamics. For example, Chapter One provides a foundational knowledge base for understanding narcissism in general. The following chapters examine specific types of narcissistic relationships.

From the *Narcissistic Mother* to the *Narcissist at Work*, interpersonal dynamics are analyzed to help promote awareness and understanding. Also included are chapters exploring *The Narcissistic Self* and *The Narcissistic Society* to further broaden the scope of awareness of the potential influences that exist today within ourselves and society.

Along the way, readers will develop critical insights that will help them navigate the influences of narcissism in their lives. The final chapter explores strategies and opportunities so that *Freedom from Narcissism* becomes a realistic and inevitable outcome for readers.

Be aware that a peaceful and stable life free from narcissistic control is possible. My hope is that this book becomes a useful guide for readers to stop wasting time and energy on the narcissists in their lives.

CONTENTS

Chapter One

The Basics of Narcissism

In Greek mythology, Narcissus was a handsome young hunter who perceived himself as so stunning in his own physical appearance that he rejected all other admirers as unworthy of his love. Returning from a hunt one day, Narcissus sought refreshment from a pool of water. As he leaned over to drink, Narcissus found his reflection in the water and fell instantly in love.

There are many variations of this ancient legend, but in the end Narcissus' own demise was inevitable. As the legend continued, the actual body of the hunter disappeared, and in its place only a single beautiful narcissus flower remained.

Given the mythological symbolism of the hunter Narcissus, it's impossible to ignore the obvious similarities in our society that cultivates, breeds, and ultimately rewards narcissistic behaviors.

The diagnostic label of Narcissistic Personality Disorder (NPD) is used to formally categorize individuals with particular traits for treatment in clinical settings. Narcissism itself can be found in various degrees of intensity for individuals that may or may not warrant a formal clinical diagnosis.

This book is intended to help those who want to feel free of the negative bondage with someone who demonstrates narcissistic characteristics. For the purposes of clarity and consistency, the terms "narcissist" and "narcissistic" are used consistently throughout this book in an effort not to diagnose, but rather to educate and inform readers.

PERSONALITY TRAITS AND
BEHAVIORAL PATTERNS

Narcissists tend to be preoccupied with themselves and their appearance. There is an exaggerated sense of self-importance, and a need for excessive admiration from others. Lack of empathy for the feelings of others is also common for narcissists.

Narcissists carry a strong tendency to deflect responsibility and place blame onto others. With this, they can be threatened by the success and accomplishments of those around them and tend to be extremely jealous. Despite an exterior persona of grandiosity and superiority, narcissists are deeply insecure. They are hypersensitive to criticism, and constructive feedback is often misperceived as unjust criticism.

The destructive nature of narcissists is most obvious in their interpersonal relationships. Narcissists spend a great deal of energy directed at controlling and manipulating relationships and have many tools for creating conflict and suffering.

Narcissistic Supply

Narcissists live off the attention they receive from others. The attention that they seek from others is referred to as *narcissistic supply*. Along with gaining attention, the term can also include sex, money, social climbing opportunities, adoration, etc.

Be aware that there always a purpose, because relationships are purely transactional for the narcissist. When one source of supply dries up, the narcissist moves on to find another.

Scapegoating

Scapegoating is an effective way to control relationships. Fabricating lies, revealing secrets, or other forms of betraying you are common for narcissists attempting to isolate you from others. In the workplace, scapegoating behaviors inevitably contribute to a miserable professional culture. In a family system, it can be toxic and has the potential consequence of being carried over into future generations.

The more lies that are told about the person who is being excluded, the more threatening it becomes to the narcissist. The narcissist cannot risk having their lies revealed, so they must continue to feed energy into the conflict. Especially if there is money involved, know that the narcissist has been positioning themselves for a long time even without your awareness.

You may expect scenarios where the narcissist excludes you from key decisions, or maybe provides you with inaccurate information in order to gain your blind endorsement. If you have ever engaged in a bit of negative gossip with a narcissist, know for a certainty that it will be shared directly with the target of the gossip even if it was the narcissist that instigated it. If you mind you own business entirely, it won't matter. Be prepared for them to artificially create statements that will be attributed to you—behind your back of course.

Story-Crafting and Lies

The fabricated stories of narcissists often contain grains of truth, and the false information added into it is believable enough to be effective. One of the most crazy-making behaviors in narcissists is the way they can simply create their own stories and pass it off as truth. It's not as clear cut as a simple isolated lie or exaggeration. That would be so much easier for us to understand.

Instead, narcissists come up with extremely well-crafted explanations for anything that will support their agenda. *Remember you said . . .* or *Remember we talked about this, and you were totally fine with it?*

Of course, you don't remember any such thing, and struggle to find some grain of truth. You might ask yourself, *Could I have said that and just don't remember?* Unless this is a pattern that occurs elsewhere in your life—when it comes to a narcissist and the stories they tell about you—remember to trust yourself, your instincts, and your own sanity.

Splitting

Splitting is another example of something that narcissists do that has some deeply rooted implications for causing emotional damage. The idea of splitting involves an *all or nothing, black or white,* and *good or bad* type of thinking. This is especially obvious in the contrasting phases of love bombing and devaluing that will be described later in this chapter.

Narcissistic Extensions

Children of extreme narcissists are sometimes referred to as *narcissistic extensions* as they exist only to further reflect the entitlement, grandiosity, and inflated self-importance of the narcissistic parent. Problems may arise and there may be strong backlash from narcissistic parents when children cannot live up to their unrealistic expectations.

In contrast, problems may also arise when a child begins to shine even brighter than the narcissistic parent by virtue of his own talents, appearance, or accomplishments. At each stage of human development, unique strengths and weaknesses inherent in every child naturally emerge.

Emotionally healthy parents respond to these stages with pride and gratitude for their child's ongoing development.

A narcissistic parent, however, may be threatened by these emerging strengths of the child if they fear that their own inflated sense of importance will be overshadowed. The narcissistic parent may falsely perceive competition. He may react with rage, and make other attempts to devalue the child in order to regain control over his life.

Silent Treatment

If you have a narcissist in your life, you already know the *silent treatment*. This is perhaps the strongest force of control that narcissists exert over their victims. Consistent with narcissists' need to control and manipulate their relationships, the silent treatment is strategic, effective, and requires no energy whatsoever to inflict the greatest pain. The message is quite simple: *Unless you do what I want you to do, you no longer exist in my life.*

The power of the silent treatment is unmistakable. It requires minimal effort and produces maximum results. It is one of the most heartless forms of punishment, and is very commonly used by narcissists.

Sadly, the typical response on the receiving end is for the victim to be worried or concerned about the narcissist's well-being. Those on the receiving end of the silent treatment are often suffering in fear that the narcissist is not safe. In truth, narcissists are well aware of the pain that is being inflicted upon you, but until you defer to their demands, you will continue to be punished indefinitely.

Projection

Projection is very different than the silent treatment, but the effects are intense and disturbing. Projection is more complicated as it is mostly an unconscious tendency. The function of projection is to deflect personal blame of some underlying feeling or quality that the narcissist is unwilling to own. Because it is not a conscious action, it is perhaps more clarifying to offer an example.

Consider a scenario when you're in an otherwise pleasant mood preparing dinner and your partner comes home from work. He is clearly uptight and under stress. Within moments, he tells you that you seem angry. You resist and defend yourself.

Within moments, you start to scan for reasons that could justify what he tells you he is seeing. You actually start to feel angry and a more emotional argument escalates. He blames you for starting the fight and eventually you try to appease him.

Self-awareness is critical when you are on the receiving end of projection. If you are emotionally content and suddenly feeling provoked, consider that the narcissist might be projecting. Stay connected with your own sense of calm, and silently acknowledge to yourself that it is the narcissist that seems to be upset at the moment.

Triangulation

Triangulation refers to the act of introducing another person (or people) into the context of a relationship for the purpose of manipulating or devaluing the targeted person. Infidelities in otherwise committed relationships often take on this dynamic. In a triangulated relationship, individuals compete for the attention of the narcissist.

The dynamic often results in suffering and destabilization for all involved. Despite this suffering, triangles are symbolic of drama, and the drama of a triangulated relationship is often sustained indefinitely until one member of the triangle develops the self-respect to opt out.

Triangulation can also occur in other types of relationships but the theme is to weaken the victim's position relative to the narcissist.

Energy Vampires

Healthy relationships are based on sharing, mutual concern, trust, and ideally some fun and lightness. In connection to certain people, we find ourselves feeling satisfied and refreshed. In contrast, when we spend extended amounts of time with narcissists, we feel physically drained and emotionally depleted. We find ourselves speaking negatively about others and engage in petty gossip to an extreme.

There are always enemies or scapegoats, and narcissists are happy to spew venom about them in their absence. Highly sensitive people, or *empaths*, often report an actual physical experience of having their energy drained in the presence of narcissists—hence the common term *energy vampires*. There is often a symbolic feeling of toxicity following an interaction with a narcissist. In fact, the entire encounter seems to lower your standards as a person.

TYPES OF NARCISSISTS: COVERT VS OVERT

It is worth noting that not all narcissists are outgoing and attention-seeking. The *overt narcissist* is likely to meet our expectations of the stereotypical narcissist in terms of their charisma and charm. The world sees them at their best, but we may experience the negative and destructive traits behind the scenes. This is difficult emotionally for us, because there may be little if no validation for our impressions.

In contrast to the overt narcissist, the *covert narcissist* is far less attention seeking, and perhaps even shy in nature. Covert narcissists may be more passive aggressive in their cruelty. *Martyrs* are also a type of covert narcissists. They are typically seen as quiet and complaining. They are strong in playing the victim role and create circumstances where they are always overwhelmed. Like all narcissists, they don't take responsibility for their own circumstances, and will find others to target for any blame.

One example of the covert narcissist is the example of Joyce who was clear that she did not want her family to host a party for her 50th birthday. She was so clear and insistent upon this, the family skipped a party and instead treated her to a meal in one of her favorite restaurants. Joyce was clearly enraged by the absence of a party and punished her family in the coming weeks with her silent treatment.

Ten years later, as Joyce's 60th birthday arrived, the family came together to throw her a enormous celebratory surprise party. As she walked in her house and was greeted by the happy cheers of her family and friends, Joyce was even more enraged. She barely drank, ate, or spoke with her guests. There is an old adage: *You're damned if you do, and damned if you don't.* Such is the life of anyone trying to please a narcissist.

The whole situation was baffling to her family, but it's very clear. Joyce was miserable because she didn't have control. Although she was the focus of their loving efforts, Joyce was threatened and angry by her family's cohesion in planning the event.

NARCISSISTIC CYCLES

Life with a narcissist follows predictable phases that perpetually cycle until interrupted or discontinued permanently. The underling theme is control and manipulation, and as soon as you understand the phases it may be easier for you to be prepared.

Stage One: Love Bombing

The love bombing stage is when the narcissist overflows with positive attention, energy, gifts, and complements in order to win you over. In that moment, you embody all things wonderful and perfect. The relationship at first seems to exist in a bubble of happiness. Your heart is full and you feel an almost magical connection with this person that sees only the best that is within you.

Stage Two: Devaluing and Discarding

This stage contrasts with the previous stage dramatically and can completely blindside you by the sudden and drastic turn. After experiencing that intense bond of love and acceptance, you're pushed off the cliff. For whatever reason, the narcissist suddenly has no use for you.

You may feel compelled to obsess about what you might have done to deserve this treatment, but don't bother. There is no rhyme or reason to it. You were once *all good*, and now you are *all bad*. In this stage, you feel like you are a complete disappointment and suddenly have no worth to them.

This is the phase for the silent treatment, ghosting, no contact, scapegoating, and anything else the narcissist can use against you. The goal is for them to destroy you in order to artificially inflate their own sense of self-worth.

They may scan for something that can be used against you, or create something out of thin air. It doesn't matter. It is the next phase of the cycle, and you need to be assured that they are gathering allies to be joined against you.

You are so destabilized emotionally, you may question your own sanity. All you want is to go back to the earlier stage where you felt the perfect connection and a sense of personal worth. In an instant, the narcissist removed those feelings.

As you suffer through this stage, I encourage you to avoid over-analyzing the situation. Healthy individuals talk through problems either to a reasonable and mutual resolution of some sort, or they may decide to go separate ways. That is how reasonable, mature, and emotionally well-adjusted people would handle a relationship mishap.

You can reach out in an attempt to create such an opportunity, but if you are reaching out to a narcissist to initiate a respectful discussion, it is unlikely you will receive a response.

Stage Three: Hoovering

Narcissists have deeply low self-esteem and thrive on control and manipulation. In earlier stages, they are in control over you. At the end of the devaluing and discarding phase, you may be feeling stronger and healthier in the absence of this individual. If you have navigated this phase confidently, you have suffered enough and are now prepared to move forward in your life.

Meanwhile, the narcissist has been burning through whatever narcissistic supply he could find and, because narcissists cannot stand the idea of not existing in your life, your narcissist will likely return. The same person who couldn't acknowledge your existence or respond to your frantic texts is suddenly, and coyly, attempting to get you back.

Heartfelt words of love and praise might be shared. You are cautious and may resist engaging. He knows you so well though, and knows exactly what to say. You find yourself laughing at his jokes. He flatters you and you're reminded of how you felt when you first met. *Maybe he has changed,* you think to yourself.

Like your mom's old vacuum cleaner, you are being sucked in. That's okay. Just be aware that this is what narcissists do.

Your response to their behaviors is within your control. If you allow yourself to be sucked back into the narcissist's life, it's only a matter of time. This is a cycle, and sooner or later the devaluing and discarding phase will return.

This hoovering phase may be fleeting, such as quick text just to remind themselves that they can get you back. Once reassured, they may suddenly disappear again.

In some cases, you will actually find yourself back in the relationship. If that is the case, observe these cycles with more clarity and insight, and know that they will continue to cycle perpetually until you feel strong enough to make clear decisions for yourself to end it permanently.

GUIDELINES FOR THE
NARCISSIST'S INNER CIRCLE

If you stay in connection with narcissists, you need to understand the rules that govern their relationships. To be clear. narcissists don't have friends, they have fans. Instead of reacting or judging, try to observe the interactions of yourself and others who interact with narcissists.

Mirroring

If you've gotten this far with a narcissist, you already know how to *mirror* instinctively. Children of narcissistic parents are masterful at it, as they've been practicing it unconsciously almost since birth. Children learn that when mommy is happy, there may be a chance at getting their basic needs met.

Mirroring is an essential survival skill for navigating interactions with narcissists. Mirroring is demonstrated through our words and behaviors. The intention is to reflect the narcissist's inflated image back to them. If they are playing the suffering martyr one day, we validate and support them. If they are playing the entitled queen the next day, we adapt accordingly.

As long as our behaviors and words reflect these narcissists in some way, we may avoid provoking or threatening their fragile egos. As long as everything stays focused on them, we may have a slim hope of getting our minimal needs met in the process.

Walking on Eggshells

Narcissists do not accept responsibility for any problems. Along with this, they are oftentimes unable to regulate their emotions effectively. Narcissists are known to over-react with rage, and later deflect all blame onto others.

Even in stable moments, the narcissist will calmly explain that it is always your fault, and no rage or devaluing would even be necessary if you did not deserve it. *Walking on eggshells* is the common metaphor for carefully attempting to navigate the emotional triggers of narcissists. In reality, it often feels more like tip-toeing around land mines.

Empaths and Flying Monkeys

Empaths are natural and complementary partners for the narcissist. There is almost a balancing act between the sensitive and enabling nature of the empath and the self-important, grandiose, and attention-seeking narcissist.

The strengths and weaknesses of these differing personality types seem to function in a synergistic way. Therapist and author Ross Rosenberg introduced the concept of the *Human Magnet Syndrome* and noted how empaths and narcissists are so intensely and almost magnetically drawn to one another.

In contrast to the sensitive and nurturing empath who is often a partner of the narcissist, *flying monkeys* hold opposite roles. In order to feel a sense of control and significance, narcissists commonly recruit others to help them bond against a perceived common enemy. However immature and primitive, this strategy can be effective.

The concept of *flying monkeys* was originally introduced in the 1939 classic, "The Wizard of Oz." The term itself is particularly descriptive of those individuals who enthusiastically join in smear campaigns and often do the dirty work of the narcissist.

For victims of the narcissist who otherwise believed they enjoyed healthy relationships with these individuals, the experience of being the target of the flying monkeys can be traumatic. These hostile allies may not be narcissistic at all, but rather they are drawn to the narcissist's toxicity because of their own deep rooted insecurities and jealousies.

WHY?

Why do narcissists have to act this way? They have so much going for them, why are their words and actions so hurtful and destructive? After a lifetime of being exposed to the narcissistic behaviors of others and supporting their victims, there is only one conclusion that consistently seems to fit: *It works.*

For a deeply insecure narcissist with a fragile self-esteem, everything they do including the manipulations, the scapegoating, the lies—it all functions to destabilize those around them and allows the narcissist to gain control.

If narcissist's goal is attention, sympathy, money, or false significance—*it works.* Drama works. Conflict works. Gossip works. Scapegoating works. Of course, this is all destructive and hurtful to others, but for the narcissist it is perceived as effective in gaining attention, control, and power.

Healthy, stable, and well-adjusted people are likely to believe and trust others at their word. For most of us, language and communication carries a certain integrity that we all follow. We defer to the truth when people speak to us.

Narcissists, in contrast, are not bound by this integrity and sense of honesty. They are also not bound by any rules of fairness or equity. If there is a family inheritance on the horizon, they will position themselves for a larger share. It's not about money, it's about entitlement.

When you are struggling to understand the behaviors of the narcissist in your life, it should no longer take much time. Tell yourself *it works*. Accept this conclusion without further analysis, judgement, or emotional reaction. Only then will you be able to explore how to best direct your own attention and responses away from the narcissist so that the narcissistic behaviors no longer work.

THE HEART OF THE NARCISSIST

Given the level of cruelty and suffering that they are capable of inflicting onto others, it is certainly questionable as to whether narcissists possess an emotional heart that is capable of love and trustworthiness.

On a personal and professional level, I choose to adopt the belief that human beings have a core self that is healthy, loving, and whole. Any deviations from that core self— including narcissistic traits of manipulation, lies, rage, abuse, etc.—are a result of their own emotional damage.

In no way does this belief excuse or ignore the abuse narcissists cause in the lives of those around them. For me, however, cultivating compassion for these deeply wounded and emotionally hollow individuals has provided me the strength needed to make difficult choices that have led to profound healing and freedom from ongoing harm.

In the following chapters, you can explore the particular dynamics of your relationship with the narcissist in your life. For many of us, there may be insights that can also help to understand ourselves more effectively. Personal insight and self-awareness leads to empowerment and hope. Those who have successfully removed themselves from abusive relationships have expressed similar moments of enlightenment. In those moments, feelings of self-worth and dignity are sparked and courageous decisions are made that dramatically change the course of their lives forever.

Chapter 2

The Narcissistic Self

*N*amaste. You may have heard this common greeting in meditation or yoga classes. In essence, it is translated as *The spirit in me greets the same spirit in you.* The same can be true of narcissism: *The narcissist in me greets the same narcissist in you.*

We all have narcissistic tendencies to some degree. Being aware of our physical appearances, or showing pride in our accomplishments, or finding ways to promote ourselves professionally may all be examples of healthy narcissism. Being comfortable in the spotlight might also be seen as a narcissist tendency that is congruent with certain personalities.

If the common saying is true, that *we attract what we are*, then it makes sense for us to be aware of our own narcissitic motivations. We are all vulnerable to our own fragile egos at times. There are instances when we are drawn to people, situations, or purchases for egotistical reasons.

If you've been suffering from a narcissist in your life, it will be useful to reflect on your own motivation for remaining connected. The more we can clearly observe it within ourselves, the more we be able to weaken this intense bond of attraction to others.

PERSONAL HISTORY AND BELIEFS

Having one brief relationship with a narcissist could be simply an isolated and randomly unfortunate circumstance. If effects of narcissism have become a continuing theme in your life, it may be helpful to explore possible earlier roots.

Oftentimes, people we encounter in adulthood are somehow reminiscent of individuals we knew in childhood. Without even being aware, we may have developed a sense of familiarity and tolerance of narcissism over time. That familiarity we developed at an earlier stage may contribute to an ongoing vulnerability for us later in our adult lives.

In a way, we have accepted narcissism into our lives before we were consciously able to reject it. This doesn't mean that we actually became narcissists, but we could be vulnerable in allowing aspects of it to seep into our lives—and perhaps even into our personalities—as we navigate adulthood.

Perfection and Illusion

It is important to be aware of our own needs for perfection, especially in terms of our appearances. Narcissists who project an overly polished image can be very appealing. At a distance, it looks like confidence and we may be compelled to adopt some of the strategies.

This veneer may draw many admirers, but deep down it may hide a deep fear of weaknesses at risk for being revealed. From a place of deep insecurity and longing, we may crave the attention and admiration of others. When we are at a deficit for close friendships and authentic connections, we may develop a belief that we must become perfect in order to attract others to us.

Social media in particular has become a forum for individuals at risk for developing narcissistic tendencies based on weaknesses of character. Whether by use of filters, photo editing, or actual surgical enhancements, people are compelled to present the best possible image of themselves.

Of course this is a common trend, and may not suggest narcissitic tendencies whatsoever. Extreme narcissistic tendencies can develop when an individual becomes overly consumed by fabricated illusion over personal substance.

Developing personal substance and increasing authentic relationships require an acceptance of natural imperfections. People are not all good nor are they all bad. To be authentic ourselves means accepting our own imperfections, errors, and mistakes and being reasonably accepting of them in others.

When we are grounded in strong self-esteem and personal awareness, we may simply be feeling a natural need to develop more friendships. The strongest connections will be cultivated through shared activities and belief systems, rather than appearance alone.

Victimhood and Power

For those on the receiving end of narcissistic abuse, ongoing exposure may have led to adopting thoughts of self-blame and deservedness of punishment. Narcissists are incapable of accepting responsibility for their behaviors so they must always blame others.

If you have been abused by a narcissist, no doubt the blame was put on you. Over time, it is typical to adopt the belief that it was your fault. You walk on eggshells in hopes of not provoking the narcissist. Each time the narcissist becomes enraged, you scan for what you might have said or done to trigger him.

Somewhere in your belief system, you have bought into the narcissist's story that you are at fault for any and all problems. Because of this, it's important to understand the beliefs you hold about yourself and your own identity. The narcissist has been playing mind games with you and it is easy to become worn down and brainwashed.

Many people who have been hurt—or even victimized—by a narcissist may have adopted the *identity of victim*. People don't consciously attach to the role of victim, rather it is imposed upon us when we were on the receiving end of aggression or abuse.

When we allow that belief to define ourselves as victims, we become desensitized to the hurtful actions of others. *It's happened before and it might happen again*, you tell yourself.

A better belief to adopt is that you are a *survivor* and speak about yourself—to yourself—with empowering words such as *never again!* Words of empowerment, courage, and freedom must replace words of defeat, discouragement, and weakness. Being victimized does not mean that we are destined to be victims.

As we choose new beliefs about ourselves, we begin to seek out opportunities to demonstrate our personal power. We look for opportunities to distance ourselves from people who hurt us. We scan for evidence in moments that affirm our confidence.

Conditioning and Meaning

With ongoing exposure, those on the receiving end of narcissism are likely to have become emotionally and physiologically conditioned. This conditioning may be particularly intense if our experiences occurred during our childhood, when our very survival was dependent upon the narcissist in our life.

When we are conditioned, an immediate experience of intense anxiety—or even panic—occurs in response to the narcissist's shifting mood or behaviors.

For example, Mary was often on the receiving end of her boyfriend Frank's silent treatments. The moment Frank became quiet, Mary would feel the beginning stages of an anxiety attack as manifested by increased heart rate, pressured breathing, and a sense of panic.

Mary was the child of a narcissistic father. Her father's ongoing silent treatments made her fear for her own survival. As an adult, Mary became an independent woman and was not financially dependent on her boyfriend. Despite this, Mary had been giving Frank and his silent treatments extreme power and control.

When she began to understand the connection, she chose to change the *life or death* significance she attached to Frank's silent treatments. Instead, Mary reframed Frank's silent treatments as a *welcome break*. Instead of the usual suffering, Mary instead focused on her own health, her friendships, and her enjoyment of the free time absent of Frank's dramas.

The point of this story is to illustrate that we can create our own reality about situations depending upon the meaning we attach. If we reframe the situation and not react to it, our energy is free to direct back to ourselves. By removing ourselves from the drama of the silent treatment—or any other form of manipulation a narcissist may use on us—we can then be in a position to make decisions with strength and clarity.

Learned Narcissism

As noted, there is strong a functionality with narcissism in that it does work to draw attention and false perceptions of significance. Because of this functionality, it is easy at times to adopt certain narcissistic tendencies. It is a slippery slope, and self-awareness is critical to avoid adopting these behaviors.

We all want to feel significant and valued. When we are overwhelmed by negative influences in our lives, especially when we have to spend extended periods of time with them, we may become desensitized to healthy and stable people.

To be truly resilient and avoid the development of narcissistic traits, it is helpful to have role models that exude authentic confidence, kindness, self-esteem, and self-respect. These traits are—in essence—the opposite of the more superficial, selfish, and manipulative traits relied upon by narcissists.

Seek role models that more exemplify what it is you really want to become in order to feel significant. Overly enhanced physical appearance and selfishness are repulsive when compared to authentic beauty and kindness. People who lie, manipulate, and scapegoat often begin to appear evil when compared to others who are honest, trustworthy and inclusive.

Be honest with yourself about what you are really want in your life. Become aware of narcissistic people in your own social circle and reasons why you may be drawn to them.

There is an old saying that is consistently shown to hold some truth: *We are who we spend time with.* Choose your friends and acquaintances with care. If the goal is to purge narcissism from your life, it will be helpful to clear it from yourself and from those with whom you choose to connect.

Chapter 3
The Narcissistic Partner

F alling in love with a narcissist can be like developing a drug addiction. It's not a surprise that the word itself is derived from the Greek root *narc* meaning *numb, stupor, deaden*, and *leading to addiction*.

In a clinical setting, clients typically describe their relationships with narcissists in a very similar manner to the way that individuals describe their addictions to drugs. Quotes from partners of narcissists compared to quotes from individuals with narcotic addictions seem interchangeable:

The feeling was so intensely amazing . . . at first.
I can't even think straight.
It's impossible to focus on anything else.
This situation is destroying my life.
I can't stay away; I feel helpless.

Why would anyone willingly put themselves through such torment and suffering especially when it comes to personal relationships? On the surface, as you know, narcissists seem to have many appealing and engaging traits.

The Irresistible Narcissist

There is so much intrigue and excitement when we first encounter a narcissist. They exude charisma, confidence, and charm. This person seems to be the center of attention and you are thrilled to stand by his side. Early on, narcissists are so completely attentive to our emotional and physical needs and generous with their praise and complements.

It's almost too good to be true, we tell ourselves enthusiastically. Our friends are skeptical and mutter, *it is too good to be true.* But we don't listen. At first, we don't want reality to encroach upon this illusion of fantasy.

Narcissists in the Bedroom

Another big draw toward narcissists is that they are often skilled and responsive lovers. Narcissists do all the research, and take pride in being knowledgable in the bedroom. They read all the books and will do anything to make sex with them an unforgettable experience.

In terms of emotional and physical intimacy, pleasing you is unimportant. In terms of ego, however, the narcissist wants to be remembered. Whereas purely selfish lovers just want to please themselves, narcissists wants to be remembered historically as the best lover you ever had in your life.

Glimpses of Ego

There are those moments where you wonder if you heard them correctly. Can they really be *that full of themselves?* You are enjoying yourself though and he is so very attractive— *maybe that's not what he said.* You feel lucky and privileged to be in his company. It is easy to ignore the red flags. What an amazing feeling to find this lover who is larger than life—and he sees you at your absolute best.

Who doesn't love flowers and complements and expressions of this once-in-a-lifetime, fairytale kind of romance? The chemistry is intense and undeniable. *Until it's not.*

The Narcissistic Cycles

Your narcissist is irresistible during the love bombing stage, especially the first time around. It may continue for weeks or months but, be well assured, it will end. When it does, it will be abrupt and without warning. Consider Terry's story:

> Tim and I fell in love immediately. He brought me bouquets of flowers until I had no table space left to put them on. After about three weeks, Tim stayed home with his boys one night and I was invited to a neighborhood party. I declined because I was just so happy to stay home and daydream about him.

> Later that night, I sent Tim a flirty email and mentioned the party invitation I declined. He said he was shocked that he could fall for someone like me that was so untrustworthy. He said he felt like a fool thinking he could create a fairytale romance with someone as selfish and deceitful as I was. He wrote that he was going to cry himself to sleep, but knew he would get over me in time and wished me a happy life.

> I was dazed and couldn't sleep at all that night. The next afternoon, Tim texted me and asked how my day was going. That was the first of many times he did that to me.

The love bombing stage is defined by gifts and complements, gestures and inquisitive questions, and promises and full adoration. Like the vignette above, there will be no rational explanation to when and how it ends. You won't see it coming. Don't spend much time trying to analyze it, there is no point. Your partner has now moved on to the next stage.

Devaluing and Discarding

In this phase, you have been demoted from being the most glorified person—to being absolutely worthless. There is no transition and there are no nuances. You are devalued with harsh criticism that doesn't make any sense. Aggressive verbal outbursts, angry pouting, and withholding of affection are common.

As noted in Chapter One, the silent treatment is more of a strategy for the narcissist rather than a phase. It is often used in the discarding phase, in place of any healthy or respectful dialogue. It can continue indefinitely, but the primary function is to gain control and punish you. With the silent treatment, you are less than nothing. You don't exist. Psychologically, however commonly it is used, it is most dehumanizing.

The devaluing and discarding phase comes to an end when the narcissist feels like it. You can say or do anything you think might help, but it won't matter. Perhaps he has found another source of narcissistic supply, or he just isn't ready to end the punishment. It's all about control and keeping you in a weakened state.

If you have already endured this cycle, you are aware of the next stage of *hoovering*. It's both the end and the beginning. You are going to be sucked back in, and it starts all over again. When this endlessly repetitive cycle starts to feel annoying and stale—perhaps you can allow yourself to flow through the stages without emotional reaction. Without reaction, it all starts to lose its power over you.

Threats of Abandonment

If you are in a longer term relationship with a narcissist, it will be almost impossible for you to shield yourself from the drama that defines your shared lives. One of the easiest ways for a narcissist to stir up drama is also very commonly used. Like a lightning rod, threats of abandonment are very efficient for redirecting all your energy instantly toward the narcissist and away from any other area of your life.

Especially if you and your partner share a home, expenses, or children—simply making a threat to end the relationship can instantly blindside and disempower even the most emotionally stable person.

From the therapist's perspective, I rarely see narcissists actually leave a relationship without first milking the effects of *threatening to leave the relationship.* Whether or not they actually leave, it's almost impossible for them to miss out on the opportunity of having you beg for them to stay.

Remember that threats are often nothing more than simple manipulation to get your attention. The gains made in grabbing all your attention far exceed the minimal energy that is required to make the threat.

If a threat to end the relationship is an isolated incident rather than a pattern, you may want to take the bait and use it as an opportunity for both of you to focus on the relationship in a productive manner. If you are hoping to stay with your partner, determine whether the threat could lead to couples counseling or other productive strategies for improving the relationship.

If this is an ongoing, on-again-off-again cycle, it may be best to just explore your own feelings of having freedom from the narcissist permanently. Until you find peace with the ongoing threat of abandonment, it will always hold power over you.

DEFICITS OF CHARACTER

There are personality traits and other assets that narcissists lack. These deficits ultimately contribute to an extremely unsatisfying and one-sided relationship.

Lack of Empathy

Narcissists lack the ability to feel empathy for their partners. This means that they will be unable to relate to your emotional experiences. When lack of empathy is joined with complete disregard for the feelings of others, maintaining strong emotional relationships with narcissists becomes nearly impossible.

Lack of Friendships

Outside of the relationship itself, the life of a narcissist is absent of deeper friendships. They may have several acquaintances and maybe a few fans, but deeper relationships are non-existent for narcissists.

As a result, your personal friendships can be threatening to your narcissistic partner especially as his own weaknesses begin to emerge in your relationships. One by one or collectively as a group, the narcissist will try to scapegoat your friends in hopes of alienating them from your life entirely.

Emotional and Sexual Withholding

Ideally, romantic partners in longer term relationships are willing to respond to each other's emotional and physical needs within reason. With narcissists, your emotional and physical needs are unimportant to them.

If you communicate to your partner clearly your need for affirming words of love, physical affection, or gestures of concern—it is almost a guarantee that they will *not* provide those to you.

Knowing what you need to be happily satisfied becomes another area for a narcissist exert control over you. Basic relationship needs that are consistently ignored will further weaken you. Narcissists thrive off this power. As you begin to feel needy, the narcissist's power over you escalates.

Being willing to meet a partner's relationship needs, for a narcissist, is perceived as giving up control. Continued physical connection may still exist in the love bombing or hoovering stages, but sex may be used for manipulative purposes only.

Remember that relationships are completely transactional for the narcissist. Even in those cases such as mutually enjoyable sexual intimacy, narcissists will occasionally withhold from you simply in order to maintain control.

Gifts and Holidays

Early in the relationship or during a love bombing or hoovering stage, gifts may be elaborate, thoughtful, and generously given. At any other time, unfortunately, gift giving will present another opportunity to shame or devalue you.

No matter how much thought or energy you put into selecting a gift for a narcissist, you may be subject to being shamed for any gift that wasn't liked. If you give up and ask directly, you will be blamed for your thoughtlessness. Narcissists simply cannot receive presents with humility or gratitude.

It is also common for narcissists to destroy the spirit of any holiday. They cannot contribute to the joy, unity, and cohesion that most people experience on these occasions. Whether it's a major holiday or someone's birthday, the drama of the narcissist will inevitably ruin the whole day. One way or another, the narcissist's behaviors will negatively dominate, distract, and demand all attention away from any enjoyment that might have otherwise been possible.

Taking Responsibility for Your Own Choices

Consider this common scenario: A college student texts another student saying simply: *Let's hook up.* The reply is: *Okay.* One or both hoped the encounter could evolve into a relationship, but it does not. Who is to blame? The one who initiated or the one who agreed? When you lower your standard for behaviors—especially early on—you must assume personal responsibility for your side of the equation.

Never devalue yourself by compromising your standards. When you do not demonstrate your own sense of self-worth, it should not surprise you that others follow suit. If your self-esteem and self-respect are strong, you set standards for yourself and for your relationships.

Infidelity and the Narcissist Triangle

Marriages sometimes end following an infidelity. In many cases, marriages were already vulnerable and the partner who cheated was seeking motivation or courage to leave. In other cases, couples lack the commitment necessary to overcome challenging phases in their marriage.

There are instances when couples actually stick together following an infidelity. They acknowledge vulnerabilities in the marriage, and become stronger and even more committed than they were before.

When a narcissist is unfaithful in an otherwise committed relationship, it takes on a entirely different dynamic. For narcissists, triangulation is a common theme. Once an outside person is recruited, the narcissist often does not choose to leave the marriage. Instead, the triangle is formed between the three, and remains in place indefinitely.

At some point, the narcissist's infidelity may be revealed and opposed by the spouse, yet the triangle continues anyway. These triangles can be enormously disruptive to the individuals, their families, and even their professional lives. Triangles are symbolic of drama, and narcissists thrive on drama. Once initiated, interpersonal triangles are surprisingly sustainable.

Having two individuals competing for the narcissist's attention is very satisfying to her ego, and the triangle will never be terminated willingly. If you find yourself in this situation, the outcome is clear. The only winner in a narcissistic triangle is the one who leaves first.

Breaking Up

Narcissists must be in control of relationships, so trying to leave will be a complicated challenge. If you initiated the separation and your narcissistic partner is resistant, he will not go away cooperatively. Between ego-centeredness and lack of self-esteem, narcissists cannot tolerate the thought of not existing in your world. It may become his mission to make your life miserable. In this way, he will continue to control your life.

In order to sustain a decision to terminate a partnership with a narcissist, you will need to be strong and have a solid plan. Leaving impulsively or from a weakened position will reduce your chances of staying away.

It is all too common for couples to break up over a big dramatic fallout as a false sense of courage emerges. As your emotions calm down, you will likely be tempted to reunite.

With each repetition of the cycle, your own self-esteem will feel compromised. With each cycle, someone is weakened and the other is empowered. Despite whatever horrific treatment has occurred and regardless of the professional advice to the contrary, people are vulnerable to returning to these relationships indefinitely.

Health and Clarity in Your Relationship Goals

It is easy to get lost in the drama, conflict, and nonsense that defines relationships with narcissists. Maintain clarity in your intentions about the kind of healthy and thriving relationship that you want and deserve.

In secure and loving relationships, there is mutual trust, concern, and interdependency. As you become informed, confident, and empowered to create a better life for yourself, the decision to leave the narcissist will become obvious and sustainable.

Chapter 4
The Narcissistic Mother

A mother is often the single most influential person in a child's life. Whether it is a single or two parent home, the narcissistic mother—even a covert one—likely holds enormous power and control. The husband of a narcissistic mother may defer to her power by means of physical absence or passivity in parental decision making. If it is a home with two narcissistic parents, the family is destined for extreme power struggles and conflicts.

Children of narcissistic mothers are particularly vulnerable to developing emotional vulnerabilities later in life such as depression, anxiety, or substance abuse. Because of this, as children mature into adulthood, it is critical for them to understand the mother's narcissistic tendencies so that the they can be resilient of the damaging effects.

THE NARCISSISTIC HOME

A narcissistic mother sets the tone for the household. The message in narcissistic homes is clear: *There is not enough love to go around.* The narcissistic mother does not seem capable of offering unconditional love.

Narcissistic mothers tend to take extreme roles in parenting. On one extreme, they can be possessive, codependent, and smothering. For these mothers, they live through their children and cannot allow them the freedom necessary to grow into their own identities. Children may feel dominated or smothered, and lack the natural freedom typically allowed as they mature.

Another extreme parenting style is defined by negligence or absence. The narcissistic mother is selfishly preoccupied with her own life rather than taking on the role of responsible parent. This type of narcissistic mother is consumed by her own desires, and does not attend to her children's needs in a responsible manner. With these extreme parenting styles, children may feel as if they are objects to be controlled by the mother, or that they barely exist. As seen with all narcissists, relationships are transactional.

Narcissistic mothers must exert their control over the relationships in the household. Scapegoating is an easy way for the mother to manipulate her children and maintain full control over the relationships. She is completely threatened by love and cohesion among siblings, and between the children and the other parent. This results in pure toxicity among family members.

When one child is alienated, other children are motivated by their own fears of being the target. The fears prove to be justified. The narcissist mother will randomly change her mind by alternating the role of scapegoat among the children depending upon her emotional whims. Once this pattern has been established, the children can never feel completely secure and unconditionally loved by their mother.

Learned Narcissism

In emotionally stable family homes, children learn effectively through modeling the behaviors of other family members. When older siblings demonstrate obedience to rules and responsibilities, younger children will follow their lead. The same is true for narcissistic behaviors. A mother is a primary authority figure in the family. When a mother is unable to regulate her emotions—or routinely uses silent treatments or other forms of manipulation to get her way—her children cannot avoid observing and learning from the outcomes.

In the absence of other appropriate influences, children may be vulnerable to adopting these personality traits as their own. Children that develop mirroring skills in order to gain their mother's approval may be at risk for developing maladaptive habits permanently. Themes of narcissism may be cultivated and repeated throughout early development and carried on later into adulthood.

Childhood and Adolescence

The idea of the *narcissistic extension* is a theoretical term used to describe the children of narcissistic mothers. The child exists only as an extension of the narcissist. The child's function is to serve the needs of the narcissistic parent. In non-narcissistic families, the opposite is true. The parents serve the needs of the developing children. The narcissitic mother, in contrast, routinely puts her own needs before those of her young children.

Even under the best of circumstances, most mothers of infants and young children can easily become emotionally and physical overwhelmed. Emotionally stable mothers often become aware of stress and exhaustion, and seek out support or practice self-care strategies. Narcissistic mothers instead project feelings of failure and insecurity onto their children. Despite their complete innocence, children may be at continued risk for being targets of their narcissistic mother's ongoing anger and overwhelm.

As children grow into adolescence they are already bonding with—or rebelling against— the narcissistic mother. Young children who bond with the mother are fulfilling their roles as narcissistic extensions and will reap the benefits accordingly. Children who do not mirror the mother, and instead speak honestly or confrontationally about her behaviors, will be unfairly shamed or punished.

Young Adulthood

Early adult years are delicate for children of narcissists. As they become naturally self-directed and goal-oriented relative to their own lives, young adults may feel the need to challenge their mothers in an attempt to exert their independence.

Navigating this stage should not be taken lightly. There is often a continued financial dependency in terms of residing in the family home or earning a college education. During this stage, the narcissistic mother will want to maintain control over her child's life and will be threatened by any emerging signs of independence.

At this stage, developing internal emotional boundaries for the mother is helpful. Being aware of her attempts to control or manipulate you, and choosing your battles accordingly may be useful. This is a temporary stage and it is helpful to stay focused on the big picture. Independence that will come with adulthood is within reach, therefore this may not be an optimal time for confrontation or disconnection from the narcissistic mother.

If young adults are dependent on financial support or housing, this stage could be used to cultivate appreciation, respect, and gratitude for those resources that parents have provided. Realizing that true independence is within sight, it may be helpful to cultivate patience. If you have come this far being hurt by your mother, finding patience may be a difficult but worthwhile effort.

Adulthood

When an adult child of a narcissist navigates early adulthood effectively, financial and emotional independence can be reached. Whatever patterns and dynamics were instilled during childhood, being financially independent allows for ultimate freedom and empowerment from a narcissistic mother.

One option in adulthood is to cut off all ties with the narcissistic mother completely. Another more optimistic option, is for the adult child to develop healthy boundaries around the mother. In this way, the individual can decide just how much time, energy, and emotions can be offered to the narcissistic mother freely. At this stage, there should be no disappointed expectations that the mother will reciprocate with unconditional love and acceptance. The child, now fully grown and insightful, is aware that the mother is incapable of this.

In the worst scenarios, as children approach middle age, there may be a continued financial and emotional dependency on their narcissitic mother. This does not seem to be a calculated decision on either the part of the child or the mother.

At some point during the child's early adulthood, the control and manipulation on the part of the mother did not cease. The child did not see a life separate from the mother and instead clung to her for survival.

Of course there are normal exceptions to this, but in general adults develop the belief that they can and will take care of themselves in adulthood. With narcissistic mothers, the dependent adult child has been deprived of the dignity and self-respect that comes with self-sufficiency and independent living.

In these situations, where there has always been a lack of love and emotional support, the more emotionally impaired adult siblings continue to compete for signs that they are more loved by the mother. In the symbolic form of money, they continue scraping for breadcrumbs of love.

Cross-Generational Narcissism

If you are a grown child of a narcissitic mother, it is necessary to develop the self-awareness so that you can interrupt the patterns before it effects your own children. As parents, we are responsible for providing unconditional love, acceptance, and respect to our children as they pass through their developmental stages. This may be particularly difficult for parents who did not experience that in their own lives. In the absence of those internalized experiences, we may unconsciously feel compelled to treat our own children in a manner similar to how we were treated as children.

There may be moments where you reactively want to punish or shame your child, as you might have been treated yourself when you were young. In those moments, you also have the potential for pure love and unconditional acceptance.

Of course, children need feedback, structure, and even criticism at times. It is always helpful for you to do a quick check in with your own emotional state. Any type of constructive feedback is best offered to your child from a loving, helpful place. If you are feeling manipulative or controlling with your child, be aware that you had that influence, but you can choose not to repeat it with your child.

Any discomfort or anxiety around your own parenting deserves increased awareness and learning. Ongoing episodes of anxiety while parenting your children could be addressed with professional therapeutic support and ongoing development of parenting skills.

HEALING INFLUENCES AND ROLE MODELS

Being raised by a narcissistic mother may contribute to an increased risk of emotional vulnerability for a child later in life. These children may experience problems in adulthood such as conflicted relationships, compromised feelings of self-worth, depression, anxiety, etc.

Over the years, research has continued to assert the position that a child can benefit from the presence of just one stable relationship with a supportive adult. Emotionally healthy adults often acknowledge how one strong relationship helped them navigate their difficult childhoods.

It is not essential that the appropriate and supportive adult be the actual mother or father to the child. An aunt or an uncle, a teacher or a coach, an older brother or a friendly cousin—any of these individuals may have the potential to positively influence a child's healthy emotional development. Consider Alisa's story:

> My mother was always mad at somebody in the family. Even when we were little, her silent treatments would last for weeks or even months sometimes. By the time we were older, she was dating and going out to eat almost every night. She stopped buying food and clothes, as if she forget she had kids.

> My older sister, Julia, was really popular but always found ways to include me. She would help me cook a little and shared some clothes with me. It's funny, but Julia never said anything bad about my mother. She always kept things positive.

In Alisa's example, her older sibling provided a healthy and supportive influence in a home that was otherwise dominated by a neglectful and narcissitic mother. She cushioned the negative effects of the mother by stepping in to provide nurturing attention and support to the younger sibling in the home. This case also illustrates that there is no need for a support person to judge or condemn the narcissist.

For adult children of narcissistic mothers, keep in mind that you should avoid corrupting helpful influences that emerge in your life. Allow positive influences through the form of friendships and acquaintance to come into your life without having to recruit them to your side against your narcissitic mother. Instead, enjoying the kindness of others and letting go of the toxic discussions of narcissism will ultimately guide you in the direction of freedom.

LONGING FOR MOTHER

Mother's Day is a particularly tragic holiday for children of narcissistic mothers. We observe virtually everyone demonstrating their deep love and gratitude for their mothers, but all we can feel is emotional emptiness.

We are stigmatized by our shame of being undeserving of the maternal love that seems to flow to everyone but us. On Mother's Day, we blame ourselves for not being worthy of love from our mothers. Beyond that, we feel guilty that we don't experience genuine love for them either.

All children deserve the unconditional love of a mother. We may never experience satisfaction from our actual mothers, but we can still can have that basic human need satisfied elsewhere.

As you acknowledge this natural longing and recognize that as a human being you are inherently deserving of unconditional love and acceptance, you begin to open up to others that can provide it. As people heal from their narcissitic wounds, they open themselves to other nurturing or maternal influences such as sisters, friends, co-workers, teachers, etc.

There are many individuals—both male and female—that have naturally maternal and nurturing personalities. Become aware of these individuals in your world and be open to receiving their positive influences. Not everyone, of course, can assume the symbolic role of a mother figure in your life. Some of these encounters may be fleeting, such as a professor that genuinely praises you for your academic strengths, or a co-worker that acts as an encouraging supporter for your accomplishments. Once the obstacle of feeling undeserving is overcome, supportive and nurturing influences can be discovered all around you.

Chapter 5
The Narcissistic Father

Narcissistic traits such as charm, grandiosity, and success are typically accepted and often reinforced in men. Likewise, manipulation, aggressive tactics, self-promotion, and an excessive need for admiration often blend in for men in the workplace.

In comparison to females, male identities are often more strictly tied to their professional lives. Because of this, the ongoing acceptance and practice of narcissitic behaviors in the workplace may become hardwired and encroach upon personal domains. As more aggressive and dominating narcissistic traits carry over into a father's home life, the emotional destruction to family members can be devastating.

BEHAVIORS OF THE NARCISSISTIC FATHER

In terms of narcissitic traits, fathers may display more overt behaviors such as verbal or physical aggression and harsh or demeaning criticism. They tend to be more obvious in their attempts to demonstrate dominance over their children. Their outbursts of rage may be erratic and severe. Because of their inability to practice calmer, more responsive forms of parenting, narcissistic fathers create a home defined by fear or even terror.

Narcissistic fathers also harm their children through ongoing neglect. They lack the ability to feel sympathy and empathy. The narcissistic father demonstrates a general lack of concern for the emotional lives of his family members. When a situation emerges that requires support, understanding, or validation, the narcissitic father is likely to disregard, invalidate, or even shame the child in need.

Narcissistic fathers are incapable of accepting criticism or negative feedback about their own behaviors or decisions. Instead, they will likely respond with rage, scapegoating, or a complete disconnect for those who don't consistently provide the mirroring that their weak egos demand. Because of this, family members either avoid addressing issues altogether, or they make an attempt to confront the father. Confrontations can quickly become escalating power struggles with the potential for physical danger.

Expressions of contempt are also common in narcissitic fathers. Children become fearful of making simple mistakes or asking questions of their fathers. Narcissitic fathers will overreact to innocent comments with humiliating and berating remarks to their children such as *dumb-ass* or *moron.*

Narcissistic fathers attempt to assume ownership for the accomplishments of their children. If one of their children is particularly talented in some area, the father may become consumed by the child's accomplishments. The father may try to maintain control over all decisions regardless of the child's needs or opinions.

From there, because of his fragile ego, the father becomes increasingly more threatened by the child's success. The more the child shines as he approaches adulthood, the more dominating, controlling, and possessive the narcissistic father will become.

If a child does not meet the unrealistic expectations and fails to live up to his role as a narcissitic extension, the narcissistic father will respond with attempts to shame and humiliate the child. In terms of receiving support from narcissitic fathers, it is a no-win situation for their children.

The efforts made toward the accomplishment of goals are of no relevance to the father. Narcissistic fathers are incapable of providing the unconditional support and encouragement that children need as they navigate the ongoing developmental stages.

EFFECTS ON CHILDREN

Perhaps the most pervasive and troublesome theme for those with narcissistic fathers is the exaggerated importance they have with outsiders. The world seems to look up to them, but the world never sees what the children see behind the scenes.

Especially relative to narcissitic fathers, *they don't have friends, they only have fans.* In general, men tend to be activity-focused in their social and professional interactions. The narcissistic father's fan admiration can be particularly hard on family members. A hurtful, distant, self-absorbed father is soul crushing for children that long for their father's attention.

Children want to please their fathers and make them proud. Most responsible fathers are aware of this and will reinforce a child's efforts to do well, regardless of outcome. In contrast, narcissitic fathers will overreact with anger or hostility in response to their children's failed attempts. The child of a narcissistic father may be exposed to shame and humiliation on an ongoing basis.

Having a narcissitic father can be perceived as terrorizing to young children, especially for sons who may bear the brunt of the father's aggression. Children adaptively learn to scan for potential threats of aggression and live on a heightened state of alert. The erratic behaviors of narcissitic fathers make it impossible for children to relax and feel secure.

This sustained fight or flight response from the children can become a more persistent anxiety trait. Into adulthood, the maturing child may be forever positioning himself for a fight. The sustained need to remain on alert could lead the children to develop symptoms of post-traumatic stress disorder (PTSD). With the development of PTSD symptoms, the child may react to perceived triggers of threat—even in situations where no threat exists.

Daughters of narcissistic fathers may have a different experience in comparison to their brothers. The treatment may vacillate between neglecting the daughter or treating her as an objectified princess. The daughter is reduced to the role of possession.

In terms of neglectful behaviors, narcissistic fathers may withhold attention and affection from their daughters. These daughters, in turn, may longing for this attention and become vulnerable to developing relationships with narcissistic men in adulthood.

Daughters may also take on certain enabling traits in response to growing up with a dominating narcissistic male authority figure Especially in the presence of an enabling and co-dependent mother, the daughter of a narcissist may learn to passively disregard her own needs.

In adulthood, children of narcissitic fathers tend to fall in to one of two outcomes. In the first, the children learn and adopt the traits and behaviors of the narcissitic parent. Throughout their adult lives, they may recreate the same chaos and drama modeled by their narcissistic fathers.

On the other extreme, children may instead take on the passive role and seek out narcissists as partners and spouses. In either of these cases, the adult lives of children continue to be influenced and controlled by the narcissitic father.

Divorce and the Narcissistic Father

Our society has an enormously high rate of divorce, remarriage, and blended families. However discouraging these trends, many parents have successfully navigated these life transitions with love and respect for their children. If handled properly, children can be resilient and continue to thrive even in the midst of their parents' conflicts.

It would be impossible to predict what a narcissist father will do during a separation and divorce. If the father is the one initiating the divorce—or if he has already secured another source of narcissistic supply—it may be a somewhat easy transition.

If the narcissistic father is on the receiving end of the divorce, he might instead do anything he can to gain revenge and destroy the life of the wife. If there are children involved in this scenario, a narcissistic father will be proceed with his destructive attempts to gain control without regard for the effects on his children.

Spouses who are not accepting of the pending divorce may do and say anything to sabotage the process. Children are an easy pawn for these parents. When children are hurt during the divorce due to the narcissist's controlling and destructive behaviors, the narcissist uses that outcome to manipulate the mother. Rebecca's story illustrates how destructive and blaming a narcissistic father can be when they lose control:

I was the one to initiate the divorce, and honestly didn't think my husband Frank would care. We were sleeping in separate rooms for years and barely talked to each other. He made all his business decisions behind my back, and ran up a ton of debt that I didn't know about.

Frank told me he would show me how hard life was going to be without him. He found the most aggressive lawyer in the area, and the divorce lasted for years. The court gave me custody of our three children from the beginning because Frank worked far away. The legal costs hurt us both financially. I guess he just wanted control and revenge, but it was the children who were hurt the most. Frankie would always tell the kids that it was all my fault.

The Ultimate Devalue and Discard

It is not an uncommon situation for first marriages to end and second families to be formed. Blended families are common today and can be navigated in a respectful, cooperative, and loving way. Tragically, there are stories that illustrate a very extreme example of devaluing and discarding.

There are cases where narcissistic father leave their families, disconnect completely from their children, and then go on to start new families. The fragile ego of the narcissist cannot assume any responsibility for a failed marriage.

Instead, as former families are discarded and new families are created, their sense of grandiosity thrives. Oftentimes, their fans provide them praise and reinforcement which can be all the more hurtful to their older children.

The older children are left dazed and abandoned, and oftentimes blaming themselves for their father's disconnect from the family. Children of these fathers will need encouragement and support in understanding that the father's irresponsible behaviors are in no way a reflection of the child's worthiness.

OPPORTUNITIES FOR INSIGHT

There are defining moments for fathers that are exposed to information about their behaviors. As noted, the lines are often blurred in other areas of life (e.g. sports or the workplace) where narcissitic behaviors may be acceptable, praised, and valued. There may be a question as to whether a father is truly narcissistic or whether the damaging behaviors were simply learned along the way.

In therapy, I have noticed men quickly transform their roles as fathers and husbands. When *non-narcissistic* men realize how certain qualities that make them effective in the workplace can be severely destructive in their homes, they are often able to create sustainable and healthy changes.

Men who are not narcissistic more easily acknowledge that superiority, control, and domination may be effective professionally—but not personally. Emotionally healthy men can acknowledge the difference, while narcissistic men will lack this insight and be unwilling to give up the perceived control.

LONGING FOR FATHER

Every child has a deep rooted human need for a strong, safe, and protective father influence. Narcissistic fathers may be incapable of fulfilling this role adequately without the interference of their own selfishness, aggression, and inflated egos. As noted, trying to please a narcissistic father will always be a double-edged sword for children. Success or failure related to accomplishments will both lead to emotional abuse from the father.

Similar to children with narcissistic mothers, it will be helpful for children of narcissistic fathers to cultivate alternative influences from others to fulfill these basic human needs of support and validation. Individuals are encouraged to develop relationships with mentors, role models, and other appropriate father figures in order to compensate for the inherent weaknesses of the narcissitic father.

As the child matures into adulthood, there will be defining moments. It will become evident that the narcissistic father does not have the grown child's best interest in mind. Responsible and informed parents allow their adult children the respect and dignity to make their own decisions. In contrast, the narcissistic father will attempt to control the child's life forever. The more the child proceeds into independent adult life, the more he will have to put appropriate emotional and behavioral boundaries in place.

If this is your situation, you must reflect on your life and determine your own course. You can respectfully discuss your hopes and dreams with your father, but you should not expect your narcissistic father to validate or support you. Remember that pleasing the narcissitic father will always be impossible. Your successes will threaten him and your mistakes will enrage him.

Your best hope for a fulfilling life free of narcissistic control is to accept and understand your father's limitations, and make your own choices in the direction of the life you desire. Your responses to your father's demands can be communicated to him with respect.

If a narcissitic father cannot adapt to his child's emerging independence in a respectful manner, stronger boundaries will need to be put in place. If a narcissitic father refuses to allow for his adult child's independence, being completely shut out may be the only option for freedom.

Chapter 6
The Narcissistic Family

The personalities of children are always developing. Certain traits like selfishness, envy, even mild manipulation may be expected at different stages in childhood. Likewise the more appealing personality traits like compassion, empathy, and gratitude may also emerge. Ideally, these more positive traits are encouraged and reinforced by parents.

In healthy families, children are free to learn, evolve, and make mistakes along the way. A healthy family culture provides unconditionally loving encouragement and acceptance while providing reinforcement for appropriate personality traits such as respect and inclusion.

In narcissistic families, respect, inclusion, and unconditional love are minimal or non-existent. Genetics may play a role in creating a vulnerability to narcissism, yet the actual expression of narcissistic behaviors seems to be a result of learned and reinforced behaviors. More malignant narcissistic traits may persist into adulthood especially in the absence of appropriate intervention from a responsible parent early on.

NARCISSISTIC SIBLING BEHAVIORS

Across a lifespan, connection to a narcissistic sibling can be among the most hurtful of all narcissitic relationships. Siblings are our only source of shared history, and we feel as if we are on the same life path together.

In healthy families—despite ups and downs—there is always a strong familial bond. Family members can depend upon and support each other. Whatever sense of competition that exists, it falls away under more significant matters such as raising children, becoming responsible adults, and sticking together during matters of life and death.

Sibling Rivalry

Siblings may often compete with each other during their childhood, but ultimately they are on the same team. Narcissistic siblings may make it their life mission to get you off the team altogether. Narcissistic siblings feel a sense of entitlement to more attention, praise, or money. Fairness or equitable sharing is non-existent in the minds of narcissistic siblings.

Of course, sharing and fairness may not be understood by young children who have not yet embraced the norms of society. As children develop—and selfish entitlement falls away—personal responsibility and fairness emerge. In homes where there is a narcissistic culture, responsibility and fairness may not have been taught during these critical early stages of development. If selfish behaviors were enabled or reinforced by parents, children may carry this sense of entitlement into adulthood with an ever-increasing force.

Scapegoating

In families defined by a narcissistic culture, trust and cohesion among family members may not exist. Secrets told in confidence are betrayed and back stabbing attempts are common. Like other narcissists, insecurity and lack of self-worth compel narcissistic siblings to demean, abuse, or humiliate others around them. These individuals will do anything within their means to hurt and scapegoat their targeted siblings.

If there has never been adequate love to be shared among family members, the drive to scapegoat another sibling might be adaptive. If one child is scapegoated from the family, even in adulthood, the narcissistic child feels as if it is a victory.

Unconditional love, acceptance and nurturing are not common in narcissitic families. For narcissitic siblings, there may be a belief that they will receive more attention, love, or resources available to them once the other sibling or siblings have been removed.

In reality, this tends to backfire tragically. This kind of toxic mentality—where love and fairness is at a deficit—the adult life of this type of individual becomes devoid of unconditional, reciprocal, and supportive love that may have otherwise been available to them.

Struggles and Accomplishments

Most families can share in both the struggles and the accomplishments of its members. In more toxic families, the siblings cannot support or validate the academic or professional accomplishments of others. Another child's accomplishment becomes a threat to the narcissitic sibling.

Because there is such a sense of deficit of love and acceptance in these toxic families, any attention whatsoever that is directed toward another child can create problems. In the event that one child has health issues, the narcissistic sibling may resent the attention the unhealthy child is provided.

The narcissistic child is incapable of feeling empathy or connection with struggles or accomplishments of other children. Any attention—good or bad—directed away from the narcissistic sibling will be perceived as a threat to his survival.

Lying and Undermining

If you have a narcissistic brother or sister, you may be desensitized to their ongoing pathological lying. On some level, you are aware that they craft stories to support their agenda, but you still defer to the hopes of having a family where members care are honest and caring with one another.

With a new friend, it would be far easier to walk away from the relationship if someone tells lies about you or is hurtful in some way. With family members, you long to have a loving family so you may be more apt to overlook the negatives.

If a sibling is more covert in her narcissistic tendencies, she may quietly wait until the right moment to undermine the other siblings. In some cases, this may be a moment of emotional vulnerability such as a death in the family. On these occasions, where there is a natural expectation of family cohesion and support, narcissistic siblings go in for the kill. They will ultimately use whatever means they can to hurt their target's position in the family.

Entitlement

Narcissistic siblings feel a sense of entitlement other the children in the family. Examples may include vying for more than their share of the parents' attention, more than a fair share of financial offerings, inheritances, gifts, etc. Narcissistic siblings lack the confidence and self-esteem to achieve their own goals. Instead, they are the energy vampires that suck the energy from those around them.

Over a lifetime, you may have experienced lies told about you, or secrets revealed about you in order for the narcissist to gain some unfair advantage. Whatever the means of harm, the outcome is obvious. It is designed to hurt you in some way or damage your sense of security in the family.

SIBLING ROLES

The Achiever or Golden Child

The *achiever* or the *golden child* are naturally gifted or skilled in some academic, athletic, or creative areas. Achievers are motivated for success and focus energy on the direction of their ongoing talent and personal accomplishments.

The narcissitic parent views them as an extension of his or her own self-inflated grandiosity. As the achiever matures, the parent may become threatened by the success of the achiever. The achiever may adopt narcissistic tendencies, by virtue of the entitlement bestowed upon him by the narcissitic parents. Although the achiever may be at an obvious risk for developing narcissistic tendencies, many overcome this influence.

Perhaps because of his own confidence and sense of personal responsibility, the achiever may be aware the disportioncate praise and adoration that is bestowed onto him. By virtue of his ability to confidently navigate the damaging effects of narcissism with humility and confidence, the achiever may be able to serve as a positive role model for his siblings.

The Victim or Martyr Sibling

The sibling that adopts this role often demonstrates traits of covert narcissists. On the surface, they appear quiet and passive, but the drama and havoc they create is calculated and destructive. In childhood, the sibling in the *martyr* role shows an ongoing dependency on the narcissistic parent. This is welcomed by the narcissitic parent as it fuels his or her sense of control.

Their low self-esteem makes them a easy target for manipulation by the narcissistic parent. Motivated by resentment and jealousy, these children may be recruited by the parent to betray or scapegoat the other siblings.

The victim is deeply threatened by the accomplishments of others. These are the individuals that rely on their ongoing problems—always attributed elsewhere—in order to gain special treatment or entitlement. The victim is effective at disrupting the harmony of a family through manipulation, scapegoating, and passive aggression.

Even into adulthood, they are limited in their ability to demonstrate personal responsibility with money, relationships, or any other circumstances they encounter. Their personalities are defined by gossip and blame, and the only significance they seem to achieve is a result of their emotional neediness and financial dependency.

The Swiss or Neutral Child

Taking from the country of Switzerland, the *Swiss* child is resilient to the toxic family dynamics and does not engage with the drama or nonsense. From early childhood onward, these children seem to be emotionally secure and able to get their emotional and physical needs met without having to either join with or disconnect from the other family members.

As the child matures, they easily cultivate outside resources through friends, teachers, coaches, etc. The presence of a Swiss child in a narcissistic family can balance out other family members. When not around, the family immediately escalates in terms of the usual drama and conflict.

The Escaping or Individuated Sibling

When confronted with a narcissistic sibling or parent—or both—the escaping child withdraws from the other family members. Eventually they leave the family and tend to stay at a safe distance in adulthood. They may or may not continue to connect with the family, but they are aware that they are safer and more secure away from the narcissistic family culture. Children in this role are often targeted for scapegoating as their distancing behaviors make them an easy target for other family members' hostility and drama.

Narcissistic Siblings in Adulthood

Adult narcissistic siblings demonstrate superficial kindness on the surface. The thin veneer of brotherly or sisterly love can overshadow the deeper intention to hurt and sabotage you as a family member. Narcissitic siblings' fear of family unity or cohesion further develops as they age. Cruelty and smear campaigns become increasingly more extreme as envy and jealousy intensifies.

In adulthood, narcissistic siblings strongly resent the accomplishments of their siblings. Instead of putting energy into improving their own lives, they may commit to the victim or martyr role forevermore. Adopting this role requires minimal energy on the part of narcissists, but gains significance in the pity and money they are able to manipulate from others that play into it.

Adult narcissistic siblings have been crafting their abuse specific to you for decades. Perhaps they have also been crafty enough to still gain—and abuse—your trust in them. Consider Alan's story:

> My older brother, Peter, was always tried to
> keep me out of family occasions when we

were little kids, but I never gave it much thought. As we got older, he would forget to tell me plans so that I would always be left out of the loop. Or he would just make up a reason for me to not be included. He was a lot older than me so I never bothered to fight him.

We were in middle age when our father died suddenly. Besides the two of us, our father was the last surviving member of our immediate family. Peter and I both had families, and when I started to make travel arrangements for the funeral out of state, he said that children were not allowed. I don't know why I believed him. I guess I was in shock.

At the airport, I saw Peter sitting there with all his five children waiting to get on the plane. I thought of my own two teenage children he made me leave behind. It was the only time in my life I yelled at him. "Who are you trying to exclude me from? There's no one left! It's just us!"As soon as we landed, I made my arrangements to go back to my kids. I missed my father's burial, which I'm sure on some sick level was satisfying to Peter.

If you are the sibling of a narcissitic brother and sister, give yourself credit for the survival skills and insight that supported you this far. Perhaps the hardest decision point in your life might be whether to continue any connection to your toxic sibling. Certainly the family system as a whole may be a determining factor. If you have a large family that crosses generations and otherwise has healthy supportive connections, this may make the decision all the more challenging. When a family has already been fractured by a history of gossip, secrets, silent treatments, lies, or scapegoating, the answer may be more evident.

Your love and energy is better directed toward friends that can provide more inclusive and family-like experiences. Across the longer term, all families will evolve. People come into a family through marriage, birth, adoption, or friendship. People are naturally lost through divorce and death. Over generations, family cultures can be strengthened and weakened. One person, for good or bad, does not have to define a family forever.

Chapter 7
The Narcissistic at Work

R elevant to the world of business, it has been said that *culture trumps strategy*. A well-managed business culture with strong systems and positive morale is an effective force in companies. Unfortunately, the presence of even one narcissist can become a toxic influence on an otherwise healthy work environment.

In some business situations, certain narcissistic tendencies may be tolerated and perhaps even welcomed. A competitive sales force may be comprised of individuals with extreme charisma and grandiosity who are effective in gaining the attention of others. Traits like these may be completely consistent with department or organizational goals.

NARCISSISTS AND THE CORPORATE CULTURE

When one individual consistently positions himself to receive undeserved entitlements to the detriment of his coworkers, resentment will emerge. Likewise, sinister traits such as manipulating, crafting lies about coworkers, or consistently scapegoating others can be a destructive force with extreme consequences.

Narcissists, with their fragile egos, will routinely undermine colleagues to make themselves look better. Narcissists may also be effective at positioning themselves with those in authority in order to more effectively manipulate them. Manipulations such as these, if reinforced, can cause distrust and resentment in coworkers and compromise an otherwise collaborate atmosphere.

Extreme narcissistic actions can be truly undermining and crazy-making. Consider Sally's story:

> I got my first job right out of business school. My boss was much older than me, but less educated. I got the impression that he was trying to put me down in front of other staff members, but I always shrugged it off. My boss literally started creating stories about me—in front of me—that never happened.
>
> In one meeting, we were starting to plan some team projects. He announced to the staff that, earlier that day, I took him aside to tell him about my lack of experience working in teams. He crafted an entire conversation between us that never happened.
>
> It didn't even make any sense. Every class I had in college included some kind of team project, and I was actually very experienced working within teams. I sat quietly, struggling to scan my memory to see if there was any grain of truth in what he was saying. That he made all this up right in front of me was really disturbing.

As in Sally's story—along with lies and manipulation—narcissists are comfortable ignoring the integrity of language. Most people defer to the truth in communication. We speak the truth and expect the same in others. Narcissists don't follow these minimal standards, and it can be deeply unsettling to be on the receiving end.

Revealing the Narcissistic Colleague

Ideally, most employees demonstrate a healthy work ethic with standards of respect and cooperation for their colleagues. It may be shocking to them when they start to notice backstabbing, deceit, or manipulation from a narcissitic coworker. The person feel compelled to reveal the narcissist's bizarre behaviors to superiors. They may believe that, once exposed, the narcissist will be confronted and some type of intervention will be provided to end these behaviors.

Narcissists are far too slippery for this, however, and have likely been casting doubt on your character for some time. The narcissist may have already identified you as a threat and prepared accordingly. As the *messenger* of his or her toxic behaviors, you could be the one at risk for being ousted.

Beyond that, when a professional situation involves illegal activity, discrimination issues, or anything else that might puts you into a whistle-blower role, be sure to first seek out appropriate supports. Accessing resources for consultation—such as an attorney, a union representative, or a human resources representative—may be necessary prior to taking action.

Being Responsible for Yourself as Team Player

Remember that the traits of narcissism endure because they *do* work. Narcissism is sustainable because there is a system in place that supports it.

Especially in the workplace, grandstanding and grandiosity can be appealing to the powers that be. The drama and conflict created by the narcissist can be distracting for others who are focused on their work. Given this functionality, you may not have any control or influence regarding a narcissist at your job. The only real control is that which you have over your own professional performance.

Try to avoid being the target of narcissists. At all costs, try to avoid being perceived as a *threat* to them. Attempt to stay off their radar. This doesn't mean you need to disappear, but you might want to quietly remove yourself as direct competition.

One of the first rules in success philosophy is to be better than your job. If you are an employee, you should always carry a sense of responsibility and contribution to your work that surpasses the position itself. Narcissists don't play fair and certainly don't play by the same rules. They have no sense of self worth, and must put down others to build themselves up. You cannot maintain high standards at work while lowering yourself to compete with a narcissist's tricks and manipulation.

A good work ethic can be demonstrated by providing honest and sincere complements to others that are deserving of them. Even the most extremely disruptive narcissists may occasionally demonstrate the ability to do their jobs effectively. It might feel very empowering for you to occasionally step outside of the narcissist's drama for a moment to communicate sincere and positive feedback to him.

Bringing your best performance to your work is always a good idea even if a narcissist takes credit for your work. Why would anyone go above and beyond at work, especially if a narcissist will take credit? Because *truth endures*. It is impossible for someone to consistently maintain a sense of professionalism, a great attitude, and a strong work ethic and *not receive* positive acknowledgments.

Maintain a strong network of fellow co-workers that are also professional in their demeanor and performance. Keep a calm and competent composure. Avoid gossip, scapegoating and other games that are the narcissist's territory. Document as necessary. If narcissists attempt to make you the target, avoid going into situations with anxiety, aggression, or defensiveness.

It is always a good idea to set an intention for meetings or encounters that make you anxious. You have information about how the narcissist might behave and should not be caught off guard. Set your own intention for remaining focused on the meeting's agenda and maintaining your professionalism regardless of what the narcissist does or doesn't do.

If your workplace does not acknowledge your good work over time, or even worse— they support and reinforces the narcissist—then you have decisions to make. The narcissistic will continue to make your job intolerable, and you will need to think about securing a better place for employment. If you have been committed to improving your own skill set and work ethic, you should have many other options available to you.

Response of Leaders

Effective business leaders should always have the company's vision in mind when making decisions. This often falls by the wayside in the midst of other daily business activities. When a specific employee is clearly trying to move ahead in the company, a leader may be pleased and even encouraging of those efforts. Narcissists take this a step further, unfortunately. Because of his own inherent sense of entitlement, his success must depend on another's failure.

When people in leadership qualities are oblivious or insensitive to this trend, that toxicity spreads throughout the culture of the workplace. Employees may lack the courage to complain about the narcissist in fear of being scapegoated.

If an employee does risk exposing the narcissist, it is likely that superiors may not take it seriously. In addition, narcissists are often a step ahead of the game. If they have identified you as a potential threat, they have already been proactively planting seeds with a superior so that you could be ripped of credibility.

It is always a good idea for leadership to occasionally revisit and remind workers about the overall vision and mission of the company. These are the statements that founded the organization and the continue to guide it.

Joining staff around a shared purpose and focus can be very unifying. Narcissists are repelled by cooperation, cohesion, and shared responsibility. They may remove themselves proactively if their manipulative tricks no longer work.

Protecting the Corporate Culture

As Abraham Lincoln wisely professed: *A house divided against itself cannot stand.* A malignant narcissist in the workplace should not be given power and influence. Alliances that only serve to alienate other employees should be remedied or removed altogether. Strong leadership should always be proactive in maintaining a healthy working culture. For those who are not in positions of leadership, consistently bringing your personal best to the workplace will either influence the overall environment, or provide you the confidence to leave.

Chapter 8

The Narcissistic Society

The powerful symbolism of Narcissus dominates today's culture. We are defined by ego, images, illusion, selfies, online dating, and social media. Supported by technology and the Internet, in recent years we have all become so increasingly consumed by superficiality and ego. It's not only the images that have taken over, but other narcissistic traits of drama and conflict are also prevalent themes today.

NARCISSISM AND POLITICS

Great leaders in history have shared character, substance, and vision in order to inspire meaningful change. In recent years, our political system has been consumed by narcissistic influences. Politicians can be elected because of their ability to instigate and channel energy from those who are angry and hostile. Narcissists take the easy route and only have to stir up conflict and nonsense to gain attention. From there, they only need to sit back, relax, and enjoy the reaction they receive from it.

We must become aware of our own contribution to drama and conflict and notice to whom we give our power. If you pay attention to a candidate's speech, and all she is talking about is the opposing candidate, *who do you think is going to win*?

When candidates becomes lighting rods for all that negative energy, they will get a lot of votes. If you want to get someone out of office, put your energy and influence into more desirable candidates. When those candidates take the podium, they should only be talking about their own strengths and visions.

NARCISSISM AND THE MEDIA

Reality shows, social media, even daily news programs are defined by ever-intensifying drama and conflict. As an audience, we have become so utterly desensitized to the intensity and bias of news stations. There are at least two completely separate channels of information for news dependent upon viewers' preferences. As an exercise, try exploring both news domains. It seems as if the news is coming from two different worlds and—as an audience—we select the reality that suits us.

Like the daily news, social media has also been integrated securely into our daily experiences. People achieve celebrity status for nothing more than the drama that they create. Take any sampling from any social media site. Notice the preoccupation with photoshopped images, social positioning, conflicts, and grandiosity. Narcissistic tendencies are ubiquitous. Of course, there are positive elements available as well, but the overwhelming narcissistic influences are undeniable and inescapable. It works, of course, because as an audience we allow it to.

NARCISSISM AND DATING

There was a time when courtship was defined by two people, once introduced, decided to take steps toward getting to know each other in a more personal way. Today, dating is all about the image. Whether its online dating or phone apps, the rules are the same. We capture a snapshot of ourselves, then use whatever filters or editing apps to perfect them. Flaws are removed, and our best features are highlighted. We transform the original imperfect photo of ourself into the illusion of perfection.

The response to these perfected images comes in forms of *likes, winks,* and *swipes.* If we don't get the response we want, we continue to artificially polish the image. If we get too much of a response, our ego inflates. We get intrigued by the attention and blinded by the possibilities.

When the time comes to meet in person, the decision point may be equally fleeting: *He was too quiet. She was too old. He was too heavy. She was too obnoxious.* Although many of us are looking for love and companionship of an authentic nature, when it comes to online dating, we suddenly expect nothing short of perfection.

Narcissists are masterful in these forums. These are their havens and they comfortably dwell in them forever. They have already crafted their messages and jokes and use them repeatedly on anyone that responds to them. It takes minimal effort and is not personal or specific to anyone on the receiving end.

The online dating culture is the ultimate forum that encourages narcissistic actions of depersonalization, devaluing, and discarding. Consider one of the more curious notices that online dating shares proudly: *If you like this person, here are 50 others just like him!*

There are success stories, perhaps when two authentic people actually find each other, but online dating overall tends to be a practice zone for what not to do when dating.

Texting has become the most typical channel for communication. Long ago, a relationship might have been initiated with questions like: *Would you like to get to know each other*? Today, it's more common to hear: *"Hey, want to hook up?"* When I work with teenage clients that are unhappy or unsatisfied with this trend, I encourage them to look at their role in it.

If someone you might want to get to know better exerts minimal time and effort to get your attention, *and it works*, is it entirely his or her fault? Of course not. It goes both ways. If you raise your standards, certainly those who have lower standards will disappear. Those that have the potential to actually meet your standards for a more substantial and respectful relationship will step up to it. Your response to narcissistic behaviors does make a difference.

Focused Energy

Whether it is in politics, personal relationships, or social media—we must learn to be aware of our responses to behaviors that we do not want to continue. If we continue to respond to unwanted narcissitic behaviors—even with negative force—it will continue to dominate our culture. If change is necessary, we must learn to refocus our time, energy, and resources on the politicians, influencers, and partnerships that you want to see thrive and succeed.

Chapter 9

Freedom from Narcissism

Between stimulus and response there is a space.
In that space is our power to chose our response.
In our response lies our growth and our freedom.

Viktor Frankl

This powerful quote by psychologist, author, and Holocaust survivor Viktor Frankl sums it up perfectly: *In our response lies our growth and our freedom.* There are no other options.

We have learned that the destructive actions of narcissists are predictable. They are doing what narcissists do naturally. We cannot change them and they are not likely to change themselves. Creating change requires insight and personal responsibility, which the more extreme narcissists do not possess. Changing our response to them is our only hope for freedom.

It is possible to experience freedom at any moment. When you are engaged mindfully in some alternate activity—a work project, or talking to a friend, or watching a movie—you are probably not thinking at all about the narcissist in your life. The moment you are reminded of this person, however, suddenly you find yourself trapped again. It is impossible to go through life juggling constant distractions, and sooner or later your thoughts will return to the narcissist.

In the following paradigm, there are three areas that together offer ultimate freedom from the narcissistic influences in your life.

STAY GROUNDED WITH INFORMATION

Narcissists follow certain predictable patterns of behaviors. This book has presented considerable information specific to narcissists and their interpersonal relationships. There should be no further surprises that catch you off guard. The specifics may change, but the themes will remain. There is no need for any emotional reaction. There is no need to become an expert on narcissism and spend your days analyzing their behaviors.

Very simply stated—this is all *information*. To stay grounded in this information means to not emotionally react to this information. Of course, the *meaning you attach* to this information may be emotionally provocative.

You can tell yourself the narcissist is evil. You can tell yourself they are destroying your life. These kinds of statements reflect the meaning that you are attaching to certain facts about the narcissist. It would be impossible for you to *not* emotionally react to these statements.

A better choice is to stay grounded in the information you have at hand. Remaining clear minded and responsible in the decisions that you make in response to the narcissist will be empowering.

Be aware, even when you are most prepared, the *timing* of the narcissist's behaviors can catch you off guard. You may have developed a strong knowledge base and understanding about narcissism. You may have even cultivated a sense of compassion for them as weak, emotionally damaged, or at a lack for having the capacity for higher level interactions.

Because of these insights, you may have become resilient to their malicious behaviors.

Be aware that the most sinister of narcissists can be extremely patient in waiting for their target to let their guard down. Narcissists position themselves to do the most damage when their targets are at their most vulnerable.

Again, without judgment or ongoing emotional attachment to these facts, it all just becomes information. For some narcissists, you will never be able to trust them to not hurt you. Remember this simply as basic information with calm composure. The next time they attempt to persuade you into trusting them, remind yourself—without judgment or upset—that they are simply not trustworthy.

FINDING STRENGTH THROUGH COPING STRATEGIES

Whether or not you decide to keep the narcissist in your life, you will need coping strategies. Staying with a narcissist will be depleting, and trying to disconnect from a narcissist will also be challenging. Narcissists weaken others in order to build themselves up. Coping strategies will help you build your strength and confidence to navigate the toxicity of the narcissist in a healthy manner.

As you practice these strategies and gain strength, you may think to yourself: *I know I can handle this. But do I really want to live this way?* Exactly. Pay attention to these emerging insights as they can lead you to clarity in decision making when the time comes.

Boundaries, Boundaries, Boundaries

Boundaries are essential for anyone associating with a narcissist in any way. Without boundaries, there will be pain, resentment, and helplessness. With boundaries, you allow yourself the safe space that is determined by your own design.

Boundaries can be external or internal. External boundaries might be telling a narcissistic co-worker that you can't take their phone calls after 6pm. Of course, they will call you at 6:15 to push that boundary. It's up to you whether you choose to reinforce the limits that you set.

Another external boundary may be distancing yourself from toxic family members. Instead of exposing yourself to their harm, you may decline invitations to visit and instead send an occasional greeting card. You avoid a more dramatic disconnection, and the message you send will be clear.

Internal boundaries involve protecting and managing one's deeper emotions. For example, a young man is vulnerable to jealousy and his narcissistic girlfriend casually mentions an email she got from a former lover. Regardless of the outcome, she may be pushing his buttons. Having internal boundaries may allow the boyfriend to avoid overreacting to her provocation.

Having strong internal boundaries will be helpful if the relationship is on the verge of ending, but you are not yet strong enough to leave. With awareness of internal boundaries, you realize that you can emotionally begin to leave the relationship before you physically are able to leave.

The Only Winning Move

You can't beat narcissists at their toxic games. There is a perfect and relevant quote from the science fiction thriller *War Games*. In the film, a computer is programmed to run military simulations in an effort to provide the best course of attack. After running through all possible solutions, the computer concludes . . . . *A strange game. The only wining move is not to play.*

When you react emotionally to a narcissist's provocation, you instantly give him power over you. Narcissists enjoy pushing your buttons and are well-satisfied when you react. There are better responses available to you. The best response oftentimes with a narcissist is no response.

Observe your emotions over time as you stop reacting to the conflict and drama that narcissists attempt to create. If you don't contribute to it emotionally and instead learn to remain calm and grounded, the drama and nonsense eventually becomes old and stale. Always remind yourself: *The only winning move is not to play.*

Observe Without Reaction

When you learn to observe without reaction, this becomes your empowerment. Observe when the narcissist is trying to get a reaction from you. Take a calm breath and reflect quietly in your mind about what is happening. You don't have to take the bait. It will only escalate and you will likely be blamed.

Narcissists lack integrity and do not play by the rules. They will make up the rules as they go along. A little joke of unknown origin also sums it up nicely: *Never wrestle with a pig. You both get filthy, and the pig seems to like it.*

Neutral Responses and Scripted Answers

We always have options for responding to narcissists. We can scan our lives to better understand what we did to deserve such treatment. We can vilify or condemn the narcissist for their destructive actions. We can try to reveal their actions to others.

These are all generic options available for our use. They are usually made from an anxious, insecure, or weakened emotional state. These responses may not bring us emotional peace or a sense of power.

There will be many instances when *no response* isn't a viable option in responding to the demands or provocations of the narcissist. Especially for family members or persistent colleagues—fully removing yourself may not always be possible.

It is helpful to be prepared ahead of time. Develop a repertoire of neutral responses and scripted answers that are simple and clear. In all of these comments, you are neither agreeing or disagreeing. The following are some statements for remaining neutral:

Hmmm, something to think about.
I hear what you're saying.
I don't necessarily disagree.
Oh sorry, gotta go, there's a customer on the other line.
We'll talk soon.

When you have a narcissist in your life, there may be a baseline of anxiety when interacting with them. Having prepared words handy for use may help you practice boundary setting even though you may be in fight or flight mode. There may not be any correct answer, but whatever time you can buy yourself to develop a calm, reflective response is ideal. In many cases, the point might be to engage you in an argument. You are confidently not taking the bait.

Neutral responses and scripted answers can be particularly useful with extended phone calls with toxic family members. Conversations may start out innocent enough, but gradually become more malignant as the discussion unfolds. Become aware of the line between a pleasant conversation and a toxic one. When that line approaches, draw from one of your prepared scripts and end the phone call immediately.

This strategy is also useful for extended family or social visits. Notice the point when the occasion take a turn for the worse. Having an escape plan can be very effective in minimizing the damage caused by the narcissist.

Stop Defending Yourself

Narcissists will never take responsibility for their problems. Projection is commonly used by narcissists to avoid ownership of their issues. Instead of taking responsibility, they will *project* issues onto you. This will not make any sense to you and can catch you off guard.

An obvious and extreme example of this dynamic occurs when a narcissists are unfaithful in their relationships. All of a sudden, instead of addressing their own feelings of guilt or betrayal, they begin accusing their partners of cheating. The partners defend themselves. This can continue indefinitely as the narcissists are able to avoid confronting their own issues while at the same time giving themselves power over their partners.

Even in situations that don't involve projection, narcissists enjoy putting others on defense. They can craft any lie or accusation just to put you on the defense. When something doesn't make any sense and there is nothing for you to defend, avoid getting sucked into this immature ploy.

Reframing the Meaning of the Narcissist's Actions

If you must cope with the ongoing presence of a narcissist in your life, you will need to change the meaning that you attach to their words and behaviors. The silent treatment is a helpful example to illustrate this strategy.

The silent treatment is most offensive and hurtful when we view it as punishment. We may scan our behaviors to determine what we did to deserve such dehumanizing treatment. Having no control over this situation can lead to intense feelings of helplessness and hopelessness. These feelings may provide a chain reaction that can lead to depression unless we can change the meaning. In many cases, perceptions of the silent treatment might be reframed as a welcome respite from the narcissist.

Accept that this is how narcissists behave sometimes, and avoid reacting or appeasing. If the narcissist wants to brood, allow it. Enjoy the freedom of time and space. This is not a surprise. Your agonizing reaction and feelings of guilt are what gives the silent treatment its power. Change the meaning and respond accordingly.

Mirroring as Necessary

Mirroring is a dependable strategy to avoid provoking the potential wrath of a narcissist. Mirroring involves reflecting back the words, the mannerisms, and the illusions narcissists try to convey about themselves.

Mirroring is a common social skill used in order to gain rapport with individuals. Between confrontation and mirroring, mirroring is going to be the path of least resistance with a narcissist. If you must mirror the narcissist, believe that you are not surrendering in defeat but rather you are proactively trying to navigate their unstable emotions.

The Lens of Positive Reinforcement

Early in my career, I worked with school-aged children with severe behavioral problems. These students were a drain on families and teachers alike, and even discussions about them seemed to bring out the worst in the adults in their lives. Many of the staff were burned out by the consistently destructive behaviors of the students. It became almost impossible to notice any appropriate behaviors in these children.

One of the most helpful strategies we came up for these students was to *catch them doing good*. This can also apply to narcissists. To practice this strategy, imagine that you are given a special lens. All you can see through that lens are positive behaviors. Anything toxic or provocative or demeaning are blocked through this special lens. Because these negative behavior are blocked, there are no triggers to your emotions.

Through this special lens you can only see positive behaviors, however minimal they may be. Random gestures of kindness or appropriate words are now obvious and stand out clearly to you. You cannot help but notice and respond to these positive words and behaviors. This is a bit over-idealized, but keep this strategy in mind to practice for a day or for a weekend. Change the way in which you view the narcissist.

Regardless of how how negative or toxic narcissists may be to us much of the time, sooner or later there might be a glimpse of kindness or normality. Try not to miss those moments.

Given that the depths of narcissism are grounded in profound insecurity, the occasional reinforcement of a genuinely positive behavior or interaction might be helpful. When we are constantly in a fight or flight mode with a narcissist, it may be hard for us to let our guard down in order to notice anything non-abusive.

If your decision is to stay with the narcissist, you will need any strategies you can muster. Conditioning yourself to be aware of positive interactions may give you some brief relief.

Additionally, it can feel very empowering when you are able to offer genuine support for positive behaviors. Consider the example of a teacher who reinforces a young bully for one random day of kindness toward his classmates. Especially for younger people, or those with more milder narcissistic tendencies, providing consistent reinforcement for healthy behaviors may lead to lasting changes.

Being All In

After spending considerable time with narcissists, it is virtually impossible to come out on the other side being our best selves. In some way, we have been compromised. Our self-esteem, our emotional stability, our ability to trust ourselves and our own judgment—these essential qualities that define ourselves have all been compromised.

Based on everything learned up to this point, there is an opportunity to establish a *re-set*. At least for our own well being, can we decide to implement some of this information and do our part completely to attempt to have a healthy, normal, stable relationship with the narcissist.

The obvious warning is that the narcissist is not likely to change. If you commit to change for yourself, and begin to contain the drama to its source—the narcissist—you will become clear and empowered for change.

In addition, you may have learned a few of your own manipulative traits during this time. In some ways, you may have contributed to crazy-making. For your own healing, you need to give this up and taking responsibility for whatever part you may have played in this toxic dynamic. Being free of narcissism will require you to be aware your own narcissistic vulnerabilities in order to adopt healthy relationship habits.

Contemplating a Disconnect

If your intention is to fully disconnect from a relationship with a narcissist, it is critical that you are in a strong emotional place. Threatening to leave when upset or angry will likely be cyclical.

The drama of a narcissistic relationships—and the cycles through which they progress—seem almost impossible to break free of. The problem is that people try and fail because you don't yet have the emotional stability to maintain the decision. *He really did it this time! I will never go back to him now!* You have professed this before, and your friends just roll their eyes.

Be aware of your own compulsion to make a *threat* of leaving. Be clear with yourself. Are you actually leaving the relationship, or are you just trying to manipulate your narcissist into changing? If the person is mildly narcissistic, the threat tactic might work. If it does work, professional couples counseling might help to lock in necessary changes. It also might work only temporarily. The threat might afford you some immediate attention, but after awhile your bluff will called and you will lose your credibility.

The best time to actually make any life decision is when you are in your most stable emotional state. In moments of peace and clarity, the more powerful thoughts emerge. For now, however, you may be contemplating change and have developed some insights:

You've been through enough.

You know deep down it won't change.

You've read enough on the subject.

You are tired of analyzing this person.

You want more.

You deserve more.

You are not trying to manipulate them.

When it comes you own personal growth and self-improvement, there will be one of two outcomes in the your relationship. In the first outcome, people become aware of your changes and are inspired to change themselves as well.

In the second outcome, nothing changes around you. Perhaps things even get worse. In this scenario—if your strength, self-respect, and self-worth have improved—then the decision to leave becomes obvious. It will be easy, and inevitable, for you to disconnect.

DESIGN A LIFE OF FREEDOM

If you are bitten by a pit viper, it's not the bite that will kill you—it's the venom that's left in your system. The same is true with narcissists. If freedom is the goal, you must imagine what life will be like without them. All the time and energy you directed at this person will be available for other areas of your life. Where will you direct all that reclaimed energy?

Take time to reflect on what you would choose to being thinking about if your thoughts were no longer consumed by the narcissist. Especially if you have grown up around narcissism, it may be particularly hard to imagine freedom from these thoughts.

Even after a disconnect, we often continue to obsess about the unfairness or scan through our personal history to find clues as to what we might have done to deserve this hurtful treatment. Unless prevented, this thought process will allow the continued circulation of the narcissist's poison in your life.

Practice Cognitive Strategies

Even with full disconnect, you may be stuck with continued thoughts of the narcissist. Know that your mind cannot focus on two conflicting emotional experiences at once. *What you don't want* in your life should be more accurately translated in to *what you do want*.

When you consistently direct your thoughts to the areas in your life that make you feel confident, valued, and worthy—new patterns of thought will be developed. Slowly this will become your new reality, but it requires practice.

For more persistent and intrusive thoughts, there are cognitive skills you can practice habitually. One skill is the *on/off switch.*

The on/on switch strategy involves visualizing a giant light switch. When you find yourself obsessing about the narcissist in your life, you redirect your thoughts to the image of this switch. You imagine the switch being turned off and imagine hearing the distinct sound of a *click.*

A similar cognitive strategy to interrupt obsessive or ruminating thoughts involves a *giant black X.* When you feel as it you absolutely cannot stop thinking about the narcissist, think and hear loudly in your mind—*CANCEL!!!* As you invite this thought, imagine a giant black X over your head.

For both of these exercises, it is critical to follow with efforts to redirect your thoughts to some other topic. Ideally, you choose to bring yourself back to the present moment. Simply take a calming breath and gently redirect your awareness back to this moment.

In this moment, are reading a book. At other times, you may be working on a project, or spending time with a loved one. When you consistently choose to interrupt your intrusive thoughts about the narcissist and redirect your thoughts to something healthier, you begin to feel free. The patterns you have now are well ingrained, so be aware that these cognitive skills will take ongoing practice for them to feel easy and natural.

It is your responsibility to direct your mind to those thoughts and experiences that bring you strength *most of the time* so that you can move forward.

You may be feeling defensive at this point. *It's not my fault! Why should I be the one to change? It's the narcissist's problem.* While that may be completely true, the narcissist is not going to change spontaneously. The narcissist is not likely to *ever* change. Your freedom cannot be contingent on the unlikelihood that they will ever change.

You can analyze the narcissist forevermore, but that will leave you under their control. Sooner or later the narcissist may leave you for another source of supply and it will seem completely unfair to you that they can continue to get away with these behaviors. It is critical to let go of the emotional attachment to the ideas of right and wrong when it comes to narcissism. Of course it's wrong, but it does work to control people. Don't allow it to work in ruining your life.

No Contact

The no contact rule is a strategy commonly found in pop psychology today. Although it is a relative clear cut strategy, the potential outcomes are contradictory. The no contact rule is used for two seemingly opposing goals: to get the ex-partner back and to keep them away.

In essence, it basically involves what is implied in its name. There is *no contact* whatsoever with the person. When it comes to a narcissist, know that they cannot stand the idea of not existing in your life. Using the no contact rule with a narcissist will only work if your commitment to it is iron clad.

If you attempt the no contact rule, the narcissist's reaction will be to regain control of the relationship. They will likely defer to the hoovering stage because they enjoy the challenge and are likely very skilled at it.

In the hoovering stage, as previously discussed, the narcissist will do and say anything to re-engage you. Complements, flowers, gifts, reminiscences—anything they can glean from your history together that you might respond to will be at their disposal. See it coming so you are emotionally prepared accordingly.

The other possibility is that the narcissist becomes enraged by the lack of control. Tragically, this strategy is oftentimes successful for the narcissist. If you don't respond to his hoovering attempts, he may change tactics entirely.

The narcissist may become verbally—if not physically—abusive. There are no limits to what narcissists might say in order to get a reaction from their former partners. Depending upon the emotional state of those on the receiving end of the abuse, they can be weakened to the point that they do actually agree to return to the abuser.

Because of the extreme consequences of the no contact rule, you need to be very committed to following through with it. If the narcissist perceives weakness, they will not stop until you are back in the perpetual cycle.

Don't Make Your Friends Your Therapists

The very last thing you want to do when you have a narcissist disrupting your life is to drain your friends with the ongoing drama. If you have extreme stress and conflict in your life, your friendships can be a haven for you. Friendships can and should be fun and uplifting to your spirits.

Your relationship with the narcissist was toxic and destructive. Prevent that toxicity from contaminating your friendships. If you feel the need to update them, keep it short. Having healthy, fun, replenishing relationships is what you really need right now.

The toxicity of narcissistic relationships will seep into all areas of your life if you let it. Becoming free of narcissism requires a healthy flow of influences from other areas. Keep the lightness and fun in your friendships.

Let Go of Shame

Similar to addicts with a pattern of returning to their drugs of choice, we may feel shame for not finding the strength to leave sooner. You may have believed in the ability for the narcissist in your life to change. Despite ongoing incidents where you were hurt, scapegoated, betrayed, and lied about and lied to, you chose to maintain the connection. Give yourself credit for being a loving person and trying to see the best in those around you. It's not foolish to hope that someone that you cared for could change.

There is no need to hold onto any shame from your past. Whatever it is that the narcissist is using against you, allow yourself to be free of it. The narcissist is threatened by not having control over you. Any shame you carry feeds their sense of control. Sometimes it's easier to blame ourselves than admit how hurt we could be by someone else's behaviors. It's time to let it go.

Interrupt Cross-Generational Narcissism

When you have made a decision about the narcissists in your family—whether it be a parent or a sibling—other family members may be curious. Especially for younger children— who may not have the maturity to understand relationship dynamics—it may best to minimize the explanation. Instead, help your children by cultivating strong family-like relationships with friends. Be a healthy role model by demonstrating relationships based on reciprocity, generosity, and kindness.

If you have separated or divorced a narcissist and this individual remains a co-parent for your children, stay focused on your own behaviors. As they say in 12-step recovery programs, put down the magnifying glass and pick up the mirror. Be responsible for your own parenting behaviors and believe that your influence will endure.

The narcissistic parent may be more demanding and dominating. This may illicit feelings of weakness on your part, but stay strong. Commit to being your best self as a parent. Maintain your dignity and self-respect with your children.

Follow your instincts while making sure you are managing your emotional stability effectively. Avoid giving your energy away in efforts to expose the narcissitic parent. Believe that positive influences will endure and commit yourself to being that influence in your own children's lives.

Professional Support

Most of the clients I've seen over the course of my career were on the receiving end of narcissism—not the narcissists themselves. The narcissist does the damage, and the people they hurt are the ones that feel crazy. *Know that you're not crazy.* Acknowledge that you possess the sensitivity, personal insight, and self-awareness that narcissists do not.

Therapists are particularly useful for those of us that are uncomfortable in seeking support. We may be uncomfortable in asking for what we need or even identifying what we might need.

People who are sensitive and giving are more likely to be the partners of narcissists. Going to a therapist can help you understand yourself, your needs, and how to get those needs met from others in healthy ways.

If you've been exposed to narcissists, you are very comfortable giving your attention over to someone that selfishly takes it away. You need to learn how to receive, otherwise you will only exist to serve the narcissist in your life forevermore.

If a narcissist pushes your buttons and knows how to get a reaction, therapy can help you be aware of those buttons. If you have certain sensitivities or insecurities about yourself, acknowledging and resolving them will take away the power from the narcissist. When this power is taken away from them, it is returned to you as the rightful owner.

There is a saying, *wherever you go — there you are.* This refers completely to relationships. The lessons you fail to learn in this relationship will continue to haunt you in future ones.

Therapist offices are healing spaces. When you offer your problems to a therapist, you are taking responsibility and giving problems the focus necessary to resolve and let go of them. Knowing that you have created a space and opportunity to talk about these issues helps structure yourself so the rest of the time is freed up for the productive areas of your life.

Compassion

My professional and personal experiences with narcissists have led me to adopt a belief that, for most people, there is a healthy core self that is capable of love and kindness. You may have experiences moments when you have felt completely connected to a narcissist.   My belief is that—in that moment— you are connecting with that healthy core self of the individual. When narcissists resort to more abusive ways, that reveals their emotional damage.

Many professional resources would suggest that narcissists are incapable of love. Especially in the example of narcissitic mothers, I cannot believe that any mother lacks the ability to love her children. I also believe that about romantic partnerships. Those moments of genuine emotional connection may be a glimpse at the undamaged core self of the narcissist.

This belief may provide comfort and reassurance for people who are committed to loving the narcissists in their lives. I choose to believe that the best and essentially healthy part of the narcissist is occasionally revealed, but otherwise it is mostly overshadowed by intensely damaged personality traits.

Having compassion for someone that is damaged may bring you strength. Compassion should not be misconstrued as tolerance for abusive behaviors. Compassion may involve distancing or a total disconnect. The more anger, hatred, fear, or instability you feel for the narcissist in your life is a signal to distance yourself to the safest physical and emotional place possible.

Whatever the outcome of the relationship, be connected to the kindness and love you possess as you set firm and impenetrable boundaries. You can completely let go with love in your heart or you can maintain whatever boundaries are necessary in order for you to love them more easily. Whether you choose to stay or to go, do not let the narcissist turn you into something you are not.

ULTIMATE FREEDOM AND
A FINAL LESSON FROM NARCISSUS

We learned a great deal from the beautiful hunter Narcissus. His life ended as he lived, emotionally empty and tragically alone. He died with no experience of love in his own heart. Emptiness and pain were all that was left in the hearts of those who attempted to love him. As you navigate your own life, commit to offering love only to those who can reciprocate.

When we acknowledge our own self-worth and love for others, we develop zero tolerance for people that hurt us. We instead cultivate relationships with people that are capable of reciprocal love, trust, and respect.

In a way, we create relationships of our own design, rather than re-enacting the toxic, hurtful relationships that we experienced from narcissists. With so much positive energy to give, share it with people that will genuinely appreciate you.

My hope is that this will be your last resource on the topic of narcissism. The narcissist will remain as a lighting rod for all your energy and attention as long as you allow it. Instead, from now on seek out books that inspire and encourage you. Explore personal growth and self-improvement topics. Commit to investing your time and energy toward yourself in becoming stronger, healthier, and happier. Enjoy your freedom.